Know What You Signed Up For

HOW TO FOLLOW JESUS, LOVE PEOPLE, AND LIVE ON MISSION AS A MILITARY SPOUSE

Megan B. Brown

MOODY PUBLISHERS

CHICAGO

Published in association with The Steve Laube Agency.

Edited by Pamela Joy Pugh
Interior and cover design: Erik M. Peterson
Cover illustration of pen copyright © 2022 by nikiteev_konstantin / Shutterstock (173932895). All rights reserved.
Author photo: Bree Cox Photography

Library of Congress Cataloging-in-Publication Data

Names: Brown, Megan B., author.
Title: Know what you signed up for : how to follow Jesus, love people, and live on mission as a military spouse / Megan B. Brown.
Description: Chicago : Moody Publishers, [2022] | Includes bibliographical references. | Summary: "Five moves. Four children. Two deployments to combat zones. Megan has discovered that this lifestyle takes its toll. She helps military spouses see that we're chosen for this specific time and place. Together, we'll discover what it means to follow Jesus, love people, and live on mission"-- Provided by publisher.
Identifiers: LCCN 2022034560 (print) | LCCN 2022034561 (ebook) | ISBN 9780802428424 | ISBN 9780802475466 (ebook)
Subjects: LCSH: Christian women--Religious life. | Military spouses--Religious life.
Classification: LCC BV4528.15 .B76 2023 (print) | LCC BV4528.15 (ebook) | DDC 248.8/435--dc23/eng/20221107
LC record available at https://lccn.loc.gov/2022034560
LC ebook record available at https://lccn.loc.gov/2022034561

Originally delivered by fleets of horse-drawn wagons, the affordable paperbacks from D. L. Moody's publishing house resourced the church and served everyday people. Now, after more than 125 years of publishing and ministry, Moody Publishers' mission remains the same—even if our delivery systems have changed a bit. For more information on other books (and resources) created from a biblical perspective, go to: www.moodypublishers.com or write to:

Moody Publishers
820 N. LaSalle Boulevard
Chicago, IL 60610

1 3 5 7 9 10 8 6 4 2

Printed in the United States of America

Praise for *Know What You Signed Up For*

This is a wonderful book by Megan Brown, my friend and sister in Christ. I could hardly put it down I was so caught up in the encouragement, honesty, and wisdom it contains. Written with military wives as the target audience, this book is for women everywhere who want to be disciples and disciple-makers for King Jesus. *Know What You Signed Up For* is a gift to the church of the Lord Jesus. Read it and be blessed!

DR. DANIEL L. AKIN
President of Southeastern Baptist Theological Seminary; Senior Professor of Preaching and Theology

"I didn't sign up for this!" What wife hasn't uttered a version of those words (at least in her heart)? But you didn't just enlist for marriage, you signed on for marriage to a military man. You already know that adds an extra layer of pressure, pitfalls, and potential heartache.

ERIN DAVIS
Author and Bible teacher

A must-read for anyone accompanying their loved one into military life!

ERICA WIGGENHORN
Speaker and author of *An Unexpected Revival: Experiencing God's Goodness through Disappointment and Doubt*

With gut-wrenching honesty Megan Brown gets real about the exhilarating highs and the excruciating lows of combining marriage with the challenges of military life. Her focus is spot-on—keep your eyes on Jesus, lavish love on others, open your heart and your home, accept your imperfections—and get wise counsel. Megan provides raw honesty, in-depth knowledge of God's Word, and nuggets of truth throughout this not-to-be-missed book. *Know What You Signed Up For* should be read by every military spouse.

CAROL KENT
Executive Director of Speak Up Ministries, speaker, and author of *When I Lay My Isaac Down*

Megan has written a beautiful invitation to live life on a mission and thrive as a military spouse because she is living the life of a military spouse. Megan's transparency and authenticity as she writes will make any military-connected woman feel like they are having a cup of coffee and conversation with a friend who understands. This conversation will come with both a challenge and ideas for the next steps. How do I take my unique position as a military spouse and thrive on a mission with God? This book should be mandatory reading for all military spouses, both those who are seasoned in this unique lifestyle and those that are brand-new. What a toolbox this book is!

JENNIFER HAND
Executive Director of Coming Alive Ministries and author of *My Yes Is on the Table: Moving from Fear to Faith*

Our generation needs Megan's passionate call to step out into all that the Lord has ordained for such a time as this. The Holy Spirit at work through her will inspire you to step out more fully into the calling to serve and love the many local military communities in creative, biblical, Christ-honoring ways. She provides action-able, practical wisdom that will empower you to do what only He can do through you. Fair warning: do not read *Know What You Signed Up For* unless you want to be challenged to deeper kingdom work!

STEPHANIE ROUSSELLE
Founder and Director, Gospel Spice Ministries; host of the *Gospel Spice Podcast*

Megan communicates a message in the language of the military spouse community: a message of the gospel and the foundational principles needed for living the Christian life. This resource is a blessing, as Megan and her family are to all of us at Back Bay Church.

ADAM S. BENNETT
Lead Pastor of Back Bay Church

Megan Brown learned the value of commitment and duty when she married a man who signed up to serve the nation. As a military spouse, she has made sacrifices that few other parents or marriage partners can comprehend. That makes her uniquely qualified to write a book about the joys and the challenges of following Jesus.

This book is a powerful reminder of what you signed up for when following King Jesus.

JEFF STRUEKER

Pastor, Two Cities Church; former Army Ranger, Third Battalion, 75th Ranger Regiment, Silver Star Recipient, and Army Ranger Hall of Fame Inductee;

In memory of Galen Norsworthy
and for
MSgt Keith Brown,
the man who made me a military spouse
and has given me one crazy adventure. I love you.

Contents

Welcome

Hello, dear friend. Before we dive into this short and sweet read together, I want to tell you what is on my heart as we begin.

My mind is racing with thoughts of you. I can only imagine what made you pick up this book. Maybe you are reading this as an attempt to feel more prepared for this life as an active-duty military spouse. Perhaps you have a longing that is going unmet. Or perchance, you possess a deep and abiding love for God, and you just haven't yet discovered how to flesh this love out as a military spouse. I get it.

When I glance backward toward my own start as a military spouse, I remember the all-consuming feeling of fear. I shuddered to think of the uncertainties that lay ahead of me, and I can empathize greatly with you today. I hope to offer you encouragement as you flip through these pages, and maybe a hint of wisdom.

Being a military spouse is a tough gig. The ever-changing pace of our lives makes the task of keeping up nearly impossible. The to-do list, which seemingly never ends, dictates one responsibility after another. Move. Move again. Stop. Breathe. Make friends. Make new friends. Readjusting feels like it is our permanent state of being. The big questions I'm trying to answer for you are these:

How do we live missionally—a life in service to Christ—when we irreversibly feel like we're falling apart?

What do we do when we look at our pitiful offering for the Lord and just want to quit?

When we are overwhelmed, underserved, sleep-deprived, anxiety-ridden, and grieving the last thing we lost, where can we find our purpose or our ability to worship?

Really, at its heart, this book is a sort of field guide for how to navigate the military experience from a Christian perspective. My aim is to share how we create a flourishing and intimate relationship with God. I want to help us learn to submit to Jesus in our marriages—the main identifier of our current role—and how this relationship is a mission in itself.

In addition, I also intend to convey how our mothering—whether for our own children or spiritual ones—impacts the kingdom of heaven. Furthermore, I want to pass on a few pearls of wisdom regarding the nature of our lives and how we could see the Great Commission fulfilled in our day.

Ultimately, my greatest hope is to present this truth: the gospel impacts every single aspect of our lives. Here's the rub. When Jesus spoke the command of the Great Commission, He took into account that we are broken, messed up, sin-soaked, and selfish people. He commands me, and you, to serve Him in disciple making anyway, faults notwithstanding. It is in this realization, the truth that Jesus calls us each *where we are* and *as we are*, that we can begin to run toward our God at a breakneck pace. We can unabashedly serve Him with everything we have—the good, the bad, and the ugly—for His glory alone.

MILSPOUSEDOM

I remember the first time that I saw my beloved husband. If this were a modern-day rom-com, this would be the part where the camera lens would pan away as his beautiful brown hair blew in the wind. His uniform boasted crisp lines and had been freshly starched. The black undershirt from the early 2000s battle dress uniform gleamed from beneath his collar. He appeared strong and muscular. His cap stood slightly over his well-groomed eyebrows. That boy was (and still is) fine!

Needless to say, one flash of his smile and I was completely smitten. I accepted a dinner invitation and we found ourselves deeply connecting. We talked all night, sharing our dreams and speaking of what we wanted our futures to look like. I remember admiring how determined he was to stand on his own two feet, and I respected his heart for service. I don't know if I would call our beginning "love at first sight," but our affections for each other were unmatched. Four short months later, we walked down the aisle and exchanged vows.

After nearly two decades, five cross-country moves, ten different houses, four children, two deployments to combat zones (and a partridge in a pear tree), along with a one-year short tour later, we have discovered that this lifestyle certainly does take its toll.

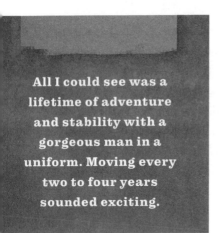

The rose-colored lenses with which I entered into the realm of milspousedom painted a picture that was so far from reality. All I could see was a lifetime of adventure and stability with a gorgeous man in a uniform. Moving every two to four years sounded exciting. His job was guaranteed. We were offered on-base housing, government health insurance, education opportunities, and what I thought would be consistency.

Little did I know just how wrong I would be. As you are reading this, I'm sure that you are smirking with delight. Maybe you, too, shared my sentiments and are now chuckling at the gross misunderstanding we believed at the beginning.

The moving was (and is) more than I can bear. Military housing was full of mold, maintenance issues, and the first place that good ol' Murphy and his Law paid me his timely visits. If it can go wrong, it will go wrong. When my spouse heads out on mission, it is a guarantee that the fridge, washing machine, or the car will break. The house starts falling apart and snakes are radio dispatched to the backyard. We aren't even going to get started on the telephone "on hold" Olympics of government healthcare. Education opportunities did present themselves, but the challenges of everyday military life as an active-duty family made them nearly impossible to participate in. Needless to say, consistency was, and still is, in stark contrast to our actual experience as an active-duty family.

During my time as a military spouse, I have battled postpartum depression, anxiety, a later-in-life diagnosis of ADHD, and a number of seemingly insurmountable circumstances. I have stayed up nights with children who have cried themselves to sleep over missing their father. I have bravely, and sometimes desperately, stood in the gap while my husband had boots on the ground somewhere else. I have been both Mom and Dad. I have sacrificed jobs, communities, friendships, and much personal comfort on the altar of military service. I have also watched as other courageous and fierce men and women have weathered the storms of long separations, bitter loneliness, and overwhelming sadness.

As an extremely immature young adult, I can honestly say that I had romanticized the military experience and viewed my future through a short and narrow tunnel. All I could see in front of me was the next immediate season. The cost and weight of my decision to marry into the US Armed Forces was completely unclear. I never could have anticipated, not in my wildest dreams, the price tag that was associated with belonging in a military marriage or raising military kids.

WHAT WE SIGNED UP FOR

There is a popular saying, a phrase if you will, that masquerades around in disguise as an encouraging statement. It rolls neatly off the tongue with sharp stings of condescension, slashes of judgment, and cold dismissiveness. It usually rears its ugly head in the midst of deeply vulnerable conversations with our civilian counterparts. The speaker, usually well-meaning, dumps it onto the floor like unwanted garbage. You probably know the phrase I am talking about, and the cold prickles are already showing up as you recount when you've heard these infamous words. "You knew what you signed up for." Ew.

This simple sentence has caused much damage and emotional pain in our beloved community. The truth is this: none of us knew. We literally had no idea. When I was twenty, the only thing on my mind as I looked down the aisle at a stunningly handsome man in dress blues was utter bliss. I had no way of knowing that there would be hard turns and bad burns in the years to come. I had no framework for the life I was building and no way to count the cost.

In much the same way, when we surrendered our lives to Jesus Christ, we really had no idea what we were "signing up for." Looking down the aisle at a loving Savior as His hand is outstretched, inviting us into a lifetime of love, rarely pushes us into a space of counting the cost or worrying about what it means to spend the rest of our days in His service.

Not knowing what the course of life looks like in following Jesus is okay at the beginning. But we don't want to be out of the loop for too long. If we truly want to serve Him, reaching those around us in His name, we have to find out what He calls us to do. Furthermore, we have to discover how.

In our time together, we will seek to uncover and accept our invitation to live on mission right where we are and right *as we are*. We will search for the passion held in the gospel, the wisdom held in God's Word, and how we can be filled up and sent through His church. We will survey all the ways we have been encouraged by God to live missionally. He calls us to be His ambassadors in our roles as military spouses, mothers—or spiritual mothers—as well as in the spaces we occupy as leaders and free thinkers.

As we press forward, we will hear His call to be radically hospitable and unconditionally loving. He will teach us and mold us to look more like Christ in our daily lives. Together, we will see what it means to follow Jesus, love people, and live on mission as a military spouse.

PART ONE

Follow Jesus

What can I say about Jesus or what my relationship with Him is like? If I close my eyes, I can envision Him walking on the beach while fishermen drag in their nets. The noise of waves and water crashing upon the shore echoes as His feet crunch in the sand. He calls to the men aboard the boats, urging them to drop what they are doing and follow Him. Quickly, they drop the ropes and nets full of fish. They shout their farewells to their families. They believe Jesus is the Messiah—the One whom God had promised. I believe it too.

The people watching this scene must have thought these few fishermen a little crazed. The hurried nature with which they ran after this Jesus of Nazareth must have looked odd at best. Placing their faith in Him defined them. Jesus, and His mission, became their life's purpose. So, likewise, it is for me. Jesus found me in the darkness, feeling around in the black for answers. He called me to stop what I was doing, put down my doubts and worry, and make His mission my life's work.

1

We Signed Up for an Intimate Relationship with Jesus

The man who made me a military spouse also had no small part in helping me become a follower of Jesus.

Before we met, I was a college dropout trying to live my best life in all the worst ways. In open rebellion, I denied God's very existence, felt extremely disenfranchised with the church, and truly believed this broken life is all we get. About six months after we were married, my husband woke me up after I had spent the previous night partying. "Hey, let's head to church this morning, babe." Laughing half-heartedly, I rolled over and put a pillow over my head to signal I was ignoring him. I said, "Yeah. That's not happening for you, man." "Please?" he replied. "I want you to just try. If you don't try, I will really be disappointed."

Well, that did the trick. As a newlywed, I didn't want to deny this very kind man an honest effort for his request. So, dragging myself from the warmth of the fluffy down comforter, I started to get dressed. I threw on an old concert T-shirt from a Bright Eyes show in New Orleans, a flowy hippie skirt I nabbed from a local flea market, and my favorite pair of flip-flops. My hair was not-so-neatly tied into a side bun and I barely washed my face, much less applied makeup. I looked nine ways of crazy. I only share the details of my appearance because it was the early 2000s and this boy took me to a very respectable, very affluent church looking like a bag lady. I'm sure the deacons there thought I needed some sort of financial assistance, and let's just say I got my fair share of side-glances.

Visibly uncomfortable, I shuffled through the pews to find a spot that didn't look occupied or reserved. Finally, settling in, I watched a rotund, stately gentleman as he began waddling his way to the pulpit. His three-piece suit was perfectly pressed, and he held this little rag he was wiping his forehead with. My eyes darted around in anticipation as he began to start instructing the congregation, a people he referred to as "Beloved," to open their Bibles to the book of Ephesians.

On the way out of our apartment that morning, I had grabbed my copy of the Bible. The only Bible I owned was the one obligatory gift Bible people give to high school seniors when they graduate. It was a brand-new, gold-foiled New International Version, and had indented tabs in the pages. To tell you how unfamiliar I was with this particular gift, I was using it as a doorstop in our second bedroom. I had rarely picked it up, much less opened it, before this particular morning in "big church." "What's an 'Ephesia'?" I asked my husband, whispering. After peering over at a few neighbors and saying to myself, *It's in the back half,* I thumbed through toward the back of my Bible and found the place.

GLAD TO BE WRECKED

The pastor started in on the task of unpacking the first chapter. Ephesians 1:1–14 is forever burned into my memory and etched upon my soul. As I listened to the words, I was overcome. God has chosen a people for Himself, a people He has blessed and called to holiness. "In love," the pastor read, "he predestined us for adoption to himself as sons [and daughters] through Jesus Christ, according to the purpose of his will, to the praise of his grace, with which he has blessed us in the Beloved" (Ephesians 1:5–6). "Beloved" was Jesus. Now, I had heard the gospel before and had a few emotional responses to a few Christian worship songs, but this time, the gospel wrecked me. All in one moment, I was simultaneously overwhelmed in the conviction of my sin and the joy of knowing that Jesus paid for it all.

After the service, we walked back to our car, and I could barely speak. By the time my husband closed the car doors, I erupted in tears. "Did you know about this? Is this true? For real?" Keith, sounding excited and somewhat surprised, replied, "I have known this truth since I was five. I am glad now you know it too." He took me to lunch and walked me through his favorite Scriptures. That day remains the first milestone in my faith walk with the Lord. On that day, I truly submitted my heart to Jesus Christ. This is where the journey for all of us begins.

That's my story. Do you have your own story of when you first gave your heart to Christ?

OF FIRST IMPORTANCE

The apostle Paul, who wrote much of the New Testament we hold in our hands, is telling God's people who were assembling at the church in Corinth (and us too) about what truth they should stand upon.

> Now I would remind you, brothers [and sisters], of the gospel I preached to you, which you received, in which you stand, and by which you are being saved, if you hold fast to the word I preached to you—unless you believed in vain. For I delivered to you as of first importance what I also received: that Christ died for our sins in accordance with the Scriptures, that he was buried, that he was raised on the third day in accordance with the Scriptures . . . (1 Corinthians 15:1–4)

The phrase "as of first importance" is tattooed in my brain. This is the most important information in order to experience salvation and the gift of eternal life. It is the linchpin.

This is the gospel. Whether you're already a believer or you're checking it out, let's review some of the basics. Jesus, the Son of God, died for our sin. He was buried. On the third day, He was raised (1 Corinthians 15:1–5). He offered Himself as a sinless and stainless sacrifice in order to bring us, a sinful people, back into right standing and relationship with God.

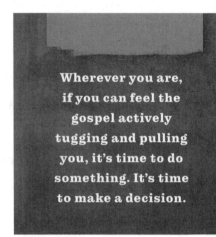

Wherever you are, if you can feel the gospel actively tugging and pulling you, it's time to do something. It's time to make a decision.

What does this mean for you and me? Well, sin can be defined simply as thoughts, speech, or behaviors that are in contradiction with God's commands for us. Essentially, we all are riddled with sin issues. From birth, we are brought into a sinful world with a sinful nature.

How do we know this? Our hearts long for things that will harm us, and we are incapable of removing or abstaining from sin in our own strength. Christ's finished work on the cross accomplished something miraculous. In His sacrifice, He paid the penalty of our sin debt and satisfied the wrath of God. Scripture says that "the wages of sin is death" (Romans 6:23). This means there is a penalty, or punishment, for the cost of sin. The gospel tells us that Jesus took this punishment, leaving us with the gift of mercy.

Now—and this is truly amazing—when God looks at us, He

looks at us through the sacrifice of His Son and views us as unblemished, holy people. If you are reading this book in your living room, tucked into the corner of a coffee shop, or wherever you are, and you can feel the gospel actively tugging and pulling you, it's time to do something. It's time to make a decision. It is time to repent and believe.

A TRUE CHANGE OF HEART

The Greek word for "repent" is *metanoia*. (The reason this is important is because the original language the New Testament was written in is Greek.) The word *metanoia* is where we get the word "metamorphosis," which denotes a transformation. *Metanoia* means to change your mind,[1] which grows into a true heart transformation. You need to change your mind about how you feel about your sin.

Do you love your sin? Do you excuse it? Is your sin something you hide—or worse, boast about? How do you really feel about your sin issues, the places in your life where God has blatantly told you in His Word that you have it wrong?

The Bible, the Christian source of authoritative teaching on who God is, what He is like, and what He wants, defines sin as disobedience of His commands. Spoiler alert: We do not get to define what sin is based on our preferences or our understanding of cultural norms. Repentance means to acknowledge your sin and to be convicted to change your mind about how you feel about them. You can't repent of your sin if you don't think you have sin.

Nor can you be saved from sin if you do not find sinfulness, or the condemnation of it, threatening.

After the act of repentance, the engagement with faith is what follows. The Greek word for faith is *pistis*.[2] Much like *metanoia*, the other Greek term we learned, the definition of *pistis* is more poetic than our English equivalent. It paints a word picture. It means to be persuaded to come to trust. Faith is not limited to an intellectual knowledge but placing trust in something you believe to be true.

What do we believe to be true? First, God is holy and is the Creator and Sustainer of the universe. Jesus is the Son of God. On the cross, the Son of God laid down His life, He was buried in a tomb, and He was raised again. He died and then conquered death in order to redeem God's people and appease God's wrath against sin. The Holy Spirit, the breath of God, is given to those who place their faith and trust in God through the finished work of Jesus. He acts as a teacher, a comforter, and He empowers us— drawing believers in toward a deeper understanding of our Savior. The Christian life is fleshed out through daily living, remaining connected to Him, repenting as we give in to our sinful desires, growing in our knowledge of Him, living in His holiness, and an enduring faith.

As a side note, repentance and belief should be shared. When you repent and believe, one of the first things I suggest you do is to call someone you know and tell them. Call a friend. Call a pastor. Reach out to another military spouse who you know is a believer and let her celebrate in this moment with you. Surely, the angels in heaven are rejoicing over you now, just as Jesus said: "There is joy before the angels of God over one sinner who repents" (Luke 15:10).

GROWING INTIMACY

Furthermore, when repentance and faith are pursued, the desire to intimately know God is present. The natural progression after we have repented our sins and believed in God's truth is to begin to seek out His wisdom and pursue a *relationship* with Him through spiritual disciplines. As believers, we should constantly be conducting an honest self-inventory and taking an active part in building our faith. The way faith is built is through spiritual disciplines, which are biblical practices used to help us grow in the grace of God, sharpen our faith, and deepen our belief in the good news of the gospel. Basic spiritual disciplines include worship, prayer, Bible study, self-examination, service, and living in Christian community.

After becoming a believer in my early twenties, I was completely starving spiritually, and I longed to know God in deeper, more intimate ways. I heard the phrase, "Have a relationship with God." Every time I heard someone say this, I would be genuinely confused. What did that mean? How does someone have a relationship with God? Many years later, I discovered having a relationship with God and intimately knowing the person of Jesus meant creating space and habits in my life, habits that visibly and tangibly represented my love of Christ. Think about it this way: As a married woman, what kind of relationship would I have with my spouse if I only spoke with him for one hour on Sunday morning? How much passion or connection would be fostered if I only made time for a five-minute chat or a passing "hello"? Obviously, the answer is I would not have much of a relationship at all.

Friend, please don't look at this section as a list of more things to do or an impossible stack of activities added to an already overflowing plate. When we submit our lives to the Lord, we "sign up" to surrender it all—our hearts, our calendars, our wallets, and our focus. All of ourselves. This submission to Jesus, saying, "God, all of this life is now for You," is a decision to ask Him to radically transform us and the way we live. Ask God to help you reprioritize your life—ordering His passions, His pursuits, and His purposes above your own. Ask Him to reveal Himself to you in His worship or the washing of the Word. Beg for a healthy prayer life and a spirit renewed. Seek out practical ways to encounter Him in your everyday routine, petitioning Him to grow you and your faith in love and mercy.

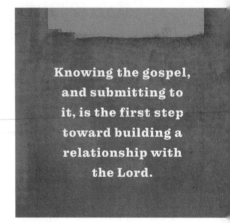

Knowing the gospel, and submitting to it, is the first step toward building a relationship with the Lord.

Here's the rub. Nothing else in the rest of this book is possible apart from the love of Christ. Everything following this section is firmly based upon and rooted in a fundamental understanding of the gospel: that Jesus died and rose again.

So, what's next? What steps should we take toward growing a relationship with the Lord? We read in John 4 about Jesus' interaction with a Samaritan woman at a well. Maybe you know it. If not, take a quick read of this chapter, focusing in on verses 23–24. These verses read, "But the hour is coming, and is now here, when true worshipers will worship the Father in spirit and in truth, for the Father is seeking such people to worship him. God is spirit, and those who worship him must worship in spirit and in truth." Worshiping God "in spirit and truth" means to worship God as one indwelled with His Spirit through the truth that Jesus is the Son of God—given for you. Knowing the gospel, and submitting to it, is the first step toward building a relationship with the Lord.

This process of growing in grace and faith looks like pursuing God with your time, your talents, your money, and your gifts. Try listening to worship music in the morning, starting your day in a heart stance of love and adoration toward God. Join a Bible study or start your day with a devotional reading of the Word. Journal through your thoughts and prayers—or find a way to slow down—sitting still regularly before God. Begin surrounding yourself with like-minded people who love the Lord, who can point you toward Him, and who will encourage you to know more of His character. Blessing others through kindness or praying together fosters a deeply beautiful bond and helps us knit our worship of God together. All these things reorient our heart toward a relationship with a loving God and builds faith that withstands the weight and weariness this military life so often brings.

Take the time to not only know God is real, that He is the Creator and Sustainer of the universe . . . but also learn to know Him intimately as Father, provider, protector, peace giver, and friend. AMEN!

Your Turn

1. Have you made the decision to put your faith in Christ and to live for Him with all you are?

2. Who can you tell about this decision, whether you made it recently or years ago?

3. Which of the spiritual disciplines mentioned are part of your daily routine? Which are more challenging for you to pursue?

2

We Signed Up for Biblical Marriage

In the early 2000s, I was a typical college student. The whole world was laid out before me, and I couldn't wait to see where life would take me.

Indifferent to most of my studies, my prime focus during that particular season was just to have fun. I worked part-time at a local restaurant, barely made it to any of my classes, and spent most of my time blowing off any semblance of responsibility. I was completely carefree.

After a few superficial dating experiences (that were headed nowhere fast), I had decided to swear off meaningful relationships.

Men were the bearers of bad news and I had made up my mind: no more.

Until one day, my passionate notion of self-imposed singleness came crashing to the ground. During the Thanksgiving holiday season of 2005, this incredibly dashing young man changed everything. He was in town visiting a mutual friend and we were introduced. Being well brought up, he was a perfect gentleman. He opened doors, pulled out chairs, and offered to take me to dinner. I have to admit I was a little (a lot) wild during those years, and his gentle nature was sort of off-putting. I had pink hair, a clip-in nose ring, and was sporting my first tattoo. He wore a white oxford shirt that was cleanly tucked into his jeans, and he had a fresh crew cut. Needless to say, I wouldn't have guessed we would have been very compatible.

After rejecting many of his advances, I finally succumbed to his charms and agreed to meet up for a casual meal, insisting it was not a date. We grabbed a meal at a local Applebee's and ending up wandering through the downtown Riverwalk in Shreveport, Louisiana, into the early hours of the morning. We talked all night. I listened to him share his hopes for the future and his dreams of a lifetime career serving in the military.

At the risk of sounding overdramatic, I was completely captivated. I found myself hanging on every word he said, and something about him just made me feel safe. Our official first date was at his squadron's Christmas party and, as I said, four short months later, we took a walk down the aisle as husband and wife.

MILITARY MATRIMONY

Sound familiar? A quick courtship and a hasty engagement start our story. We were barely twenty years old when we exchanged vows and we had no idea what it would be like to manage a marriage during wartime. Our naïve assumptions are laughable now that I think about it. In our minds, our newfound love seemed unbreakable. Theoretically, we could withstand the rocky waters of high operations tempos and navigate the rapids of living paycheck to paycheck. We wholeheartedly believed that we could escape the relationship-shredding machine of long deployments and still connect through video chats—connections that were separated by fifteen hours in time difference.

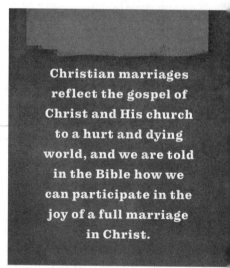

Christian marriages reflect the gospel of Christ and His church to a hurt and dying world, and we are told in the Bible how we can participate in the joy of a full marriage in Christ.

While we have managed to survive, we aren't without our battle scars. With bloodied hands and knees, we have managed to crawl our way through the battlefield of military marriage.

Military marriage can sometimes feel like a minefield, right? Combat stress, financial worries, intimacy issues, and reintegration are more than just words to us. These words encompass the proverbial "mines" that lie just beneath the surface of a would-be successful marriage. Biblically, marriage is a unique relationship.

Luckily for us, when my husband and I were first married, we joined a "Newly/Nearly Married" Sunday school class in Columbus, Mississippi. It was our first duty station, and we had found our church home. The couple leading this study were more seasoned in matrimony than we were, having been married for several years. They helped us build the foundation of our marriage. We took a personality test, did worksheets on decision-making, and learned how to become unified. Being shepherded by this sweet couple helped us solidify a biblical view of Christian marriage. I learned to see my marriage to an active-duty service member as one of my top priorities.

Let's just look at the term "milspouse." This nickname has become one of my primary identifiers in modern culture. I am married to someone who serves. I could spend all day comparing and contrasting the differences between civilian and military marriages, but instead I want us to focus on two things. Christian marriages reflect the gospel of Christ and His church to a hurt and dying world, and we are told in the Bible how we can participate in the joy of a full marriage in Christ.

If you've been in or around a local church and its teachings on marriage, you have probably heard the term "biblical marriage." What is a biblical marriage, and what does it look like? How does a biblical marriage function? Is there practical wisdom anywhere on how to live out its principles? I know that these questions swirled around in my own mind when I first became a believer.

MARRIAGE AS A MINISTRY?
WHAT DO YOU THINK?

Contemporary culture would probably define marriage as an institution one can enter into and exit out of based entirely on happiness or the inconvenience of being tied down. Or, perhaps, this union is simply a timely contract between two parties who wish to be committed to one another for the time being. I'm not baggin' on contemporary culture. If we're honest, in our post-Christian times, I have no expectation of the popular culture reflecting anything that closely resembles biblical mandates or principles.

However, if you and I proclaim to follow Jesus, our Christian marriage is one of our first responsibilities to care for and steward—especially in our hopes of living Christ-filled lives in the military community. The Bible defines marriage early on: Genesis 2:24 reads, "Therefore, a man shall leave his father and his mother and hold fast to his wife, and they shall become one flesh."

Here's a quick Bible study tip. Anytime you see the word "therefore," you can raise a mental flag to review everything that came before that particular verse. In this case, Moses, the author of Genesis, is pointing the reader back to the beginning story of creation. Basically, he is saying, "God created the heavens and the earth, the birds of the air and the creatures of the sea, the man from the dirt, and the woman from the man's rib, both in His image. Now, this will be what happens. A man will leave his immediate family, be joined to his wife, and they will become one flesh."

We see this Scripture quoted again in the book of Ephesians. The apostle Paul wrote a letter to the local church in the ancient city of Ephesus. If we take a quick glance at its pages, we will see just how this new family, a man cleaving to his wife, fleshes out in real time. In Ephesians 5:21–34, Paul writes about the marriage relationship.

"Submit to one another out of reverence for Christ," he begins. He continues, "Wives, submit yourselves to your own husbands as you do to the Lord. For the husband is the head of the wife as Christ is the head of the church, his body, of which he is the Savior. Now as the church submits to Christ, so also wives should submit to their husbands in everything."

There it is, y'all. The trigger word. Submission. Before you tune me out, know that I have much to say about the topic of biblical submission, a topic that has sadly been skewed from its intent. Submission to one's husband is not the center of what it means to be a Christian woman. Many times, when women in faith communities hear this word, they cringe because of how often this principle is elevated as an identifier of a woman's faith. Ultimately, it is the submission to Jesus that is the most integral identifier of a woman of faith.

But for the sake of time and focus, I want to keep our current conversation nice and light. My focus here is not, absolutely and unapologetically not, the age-old message of "be a submissive wife," describing that trait as the mark of a biblical woman. In fact—and this is key—submissiveness is a characteristic of *both*

Christian men and women.

As we seek to be shaped more and more like Jesus, the process called sanctification, we have to see that submission is the first command given to us *as a couple* in verse 21. This submission to the Lord is explained in the following verses. Wives, we submit to Jesus by submitting to our husband's good and godly leadership. Because this concept

> Both man and woman are created by God, beautifully reflecting His image in unique ways (Genesis 1:27).

has too often been distorted, it is important to note that we do not blindly submit to sinful requests or to manipulation. This Scripture also does not imply that this willing and voluntary submission is due to a man's superiority or to the fact that he "deserves" such a gift. Both man and woman are created by God, beautifully reflecting His image in unique ways (Genesis 1:27). They are equal in humanity and dignity. Amen.

After the apostle Paul instructs wives to be submissive toward their husbands, he instructs the married man to be radically sacrificial. He writes,

> Husbands, love your wives, as Christ loved the church and gave himself up for her, that he might sanctify her, having cleansed her by the washing with water with the word, so that he might present the church to himself in splendor, without

spot or wrinkle or any such thing, that she might be holy and without blemish. (Ephesians 5:25–27)

This is what Christ has done for the church, Paul explains. And this is the example Paul instructs husbands to emulate:

In this same way, husbands should love their wives as their own bodies. He who loves his wife loves himself. For no one ever hated his own flesh, but nourishes and cherishes it, just as Christ does the church, because we are members of his body. (vv. 28–30)

So, husbands are to submit to the Lord through their willingness to serve and sacrifice for their wives. Consider that. The Scripture is painting this picture of sacrifice by illustrating Christ's deep and abiding love for the church, even to the point of laying down His life for her. That's a pretty tall order, boys. Husbands are charged with "sanctifying" their wives through "the washing of the word" and told to "present" her without "spot or blemish." Wow. More big tasks.

Husbands are then commanded to love their wives in such a way that their love manifests into care and compassion. Words like "nourish" and "cherish" are laced through the passage. He repeats the foundational statement from Genesis: "Therefore, a man shall leave his father and his mother and hold fast to his wife, and they shall become one flesh."

Finally, Paul sums up his passage with a revelation and instruction. "This mystery is profound, and I am saying that it refers to Christ and the church. However, let each one of you love his wife as himself, and let the wife see that she respects her husband." Conclusively, Paul in Ephesians is teaching married couples how to behave toward each other *in order to glorify the Lord in their relationship and reflect the gospel in their relationship.*

Ultimately, biblical marriage is a deeply held covenant—that is, a promise—between a man and a woman to an ultimate commitment. The commitment is to preserve a lifelong relationship that glorifies the Lord and reflects the gospel. This unique relationship is the epitome of the message that Christ has an unshakable, unbreakable bond with His church. Biblical marriage is characterized and marked by both parties being fully submitted to Christ: the wife through voluntarily placing herself under her husband's authority and showing deep respect to him, and the husband through a radically sacrificial love and dedication to cherishing his wife in practical ways.

CLING TO THE CROSS TOGETHER

As a seasoned spouse, I admit to a real temptation to start doling out the advice on how to live this out in practical and successful ways. But instead of the trite "do this" or "try that" speech, I want to encourage you. A biblical marriage flows and functions because of two main components. First, the power and grace of God empowers husbands and wives to love each other out of the abundance of their relationship with Him. And second, biblical marriage takes the deeply held commitment of two people to know each other intimately and love each other fiercely in spite of their circumstances.

When you set yourselves to the task of pursuing a biblical marriage, a relationship marked by submission to the Lord and abiding love for another, first set yourself to the task of drawing nearer to God. Place yourself under His teaching by reading and studying

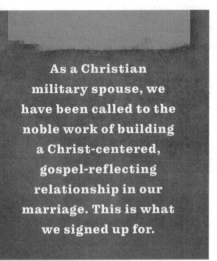

As a Christian military spouse, we have been called to the noble work of building a Christ-centered, gospel-reflecting relationship in our marriage. This is what we signed up for.

His Word. Worship more fully in your everyday routine. Develop the spiritual disciplines of prayer and community so that the power and grace of God can saturate your life and show you fully how Christ has done it all.

Additionally, make a commitment to really know your spouse. Find out how they handle disappointment (there will be much of this throughout your active-duty life). Learn how they celebrate. Observe what actions or activities bring them the most joy. Propagate a life that communicates your love for them because of your intimate understanding of their personality and their preferences. One amazing resource in this endeavor is *The 5 Love Languages* by Dr. Gary Chapman. He has even released a military edition of this book, which you may find helpful.[3]

Living out your faith in Christ through serving and sacrificing in your marriages is no easy task. And for some of you reading through this chapter, you may feel frustrated or overwhelmed because your spouse may or may not be a believer. If you are reading these pages with tears in your eyes or resentment in your heart, I've penned "A Letter from Megan" for you in the back of this book. I realize that the call to biblical marriage can feel intimidating, and sometimes we tend to avoid difficult things because of the chaos in everyday life. But, as a follower of Jesus, we are called to submit ourselves to our Savior and follow the teachings we have been given in the Word. As a Christian military spouse, we have been called to the noble work of building a Christ-centered, gospel-reflecting relationship in our marriage. This is what we signed up for.

What I have found, after nearly two decades as a military spouse, is that my husband really is my best friend. He is the first person I want to celebrate with, the first person I want when I need comfort or reassurance, and I count on him in a way that is difficult to describe. But we didn't just get here. We walked every step of the way with the intention of tethering ourselves together. What I mean to say is that hard things like deployments and reintegration have taken their toll on us as a couple, but through dogged determination and a refusal to give up on each other, we have managed to make it through.

When Keith was stationed in Korea for an entire year, we were barely able to speak for nine months. The time difference was insane, and we were sort of like passing ships in the night. He was going to bed when the kids and I were getting up. He was getting up while we were drifting off to sleep. Simultaneously, during that season of long separation, our four children and I endured some of the hardest circumstances we had ever faced as a family in his absence. We moved from Georgia to Mississippi only two weeks before he was supposed to report overseas. I barely got the boxes off the truck before we said goodbye. The kids clung to my legs and cried when we entered a practically empty house. For the next six months, I battled through building community for our kids, a task that took every ounce of my mental and emotional real estate. We all got cripplingly sick, survived three hurricanes, and managed to finish up our homeschool schedule. By the time Keith came home, I was seriously exhausted, overworked, and—if I'm transparently honest—completely eaten up with resentment.

I resented the circumstances I had to work through without any support. I was angry that every aspect of my life had been impacted by the military's decision to send my spouse to the other side of the world. Even more so, our year spent on separate continents cost our children more than I was prepared to ask them to pay. With anxiety through the roof, no shortage of tears, and gut-wrenching anguish, our four kiddos pushed through to the finish line. At the end of the short tour, our relationship had no small number of needed repairs. I guess I'm sharing all these details to say this: I get it. Military marriages are beyond hard to navigate, but Jesus called us to this specific ministry, and following Him means we value what He values.

I know this: Jesus values my husband. And He uses this relationship, our marriage, to project the story of His sacrifice to our community.

In following Jesus through our military marriages, the call of action we have as military spouses requires us to view our relationship differently and treat it with immense care. Marriage is a ministry. Our Christian marriages are not simply contracts, nor are they designed to be our constant source of happiness. We can all agree that, many times, we find ourselves aching because of the hurt and loss that comes with this territory.

TO GUARD AND PROTECT

In fact, in addition to viewing our relationship as a ministry, we must learn to guard it and protect it with vigilance. We have to protect our relationship against the things our military culture, or even our societal understandings, would slip inside it. Harmful and destructive things, like substance abuse, pornography, and adultery lurk beneath every surface. The alcohol culture in our community is running rampant. Pornography, many times, is unfortunately presented as a healthier way of coping with a long separation than cheating. Over my many years in women's ministry, I learned that this lie is pervasive and the cause of much marital disharmony and hurt.

I want to also distinguish the fact that emotional affairs count as adultery and, as military couples, we have to be aware of how quickly inappropriate emotional bonds can form if we are not intentional about protecting ourselves from this tendency. Before I get tuned out, it is vital to point out that, while the sin of adultery or cheating is not more or less present in military couples than in the general population, this particular entanglement has more opportunity to creep in because of our lifestyles. Ultimately, what I'm trying to say is that we must be aware of the challenges facing our marriage and that our ministry to our spouse includes building strong ties, fostering a deep and abiding love for each other, and holding one another accountable to walking out our faith together.

Over the years, my husband, Keith, and I have endured two combat tours and a short tour to Korea. In addition, we have navigated the rough waters of reintegration a time or two. I have learned a few things about trekking through the tough terrain of a military marriage. This task is littered with the "ticking time bombs" of resentment, frustration, and disconnection. When you learn to live apart for a season—even though it is excruciatingly painful to deal with the loneliness and the struggle of holding down the home front—the homecoming is sometimes (if not every time) harder. Merging two lives back into one home—and one bank account—is enough to make me scream. It takes real commitment and grit to keep marriages in our community running.

We have to guard our hearts, set realistic expectations, and truly rely upon the Lord to see us through. In keeping our eyes fixed on Jesus, we can move in practical ways toward growing back together and seeking Him first.

Your Turn

1. How did you and your spouse meet? What attracted you to each other?

2. In what ways have you found a military marriage challenging? Why is it helpful to find a friend or mentor who's further along in marriage and can encourage you?

3. How are you guarding and protecting your marriage?

3

We Signed up to Leave a Legacy of Faith

I often trek down the street to share a cup of coffee with my neighbor.

At the time, we were both homeschooling mamas and every once in a while, we liked to let the littles play together while we conversed with another adult. We'd sip our mugs of hot, heavenly caffeine and overhear the muffled giggles of kiddos in the other room while we discussed how we're feeling about discipling our children. "Sometimes the task just feels overwhelming" is a sentiment we shared. My children's ages now range from elementary grades up into high school territory, and I can certainly say the years pass by too quickly.

If I close my eyes, I can time travel back to the day my oldest was born. Hannah arrived in mid-2008 to the sounds of my favorite songs. Yes, I packed my iPod Shuffle in my hospital bag and made a mix tape for such an occasion. Her sweet, round face stared up at me and, in that moment, everything else seemed to fade into the background. God had given me this beautiful little girl to shepherd, steward, and point toward a Savior. What a responsibility. How on earth was I supposed to know what to do or how to go about such an enormous task? After all, at that point, only a few months had passed since I, myself, had submitted myself to the Lord in faith. I had no idea how to raise a child in the love and mercy of God.

Many years later, and all of a sudden, this bouncing baby girl

I know one thing for certain: women are always looking for someone to disciple them at every stage.

became a teenager. She flits and floats through our house, blaring loud music, and wearing colorfully expressive clothing. She is highly opinionated, vivacious, and still makes my heart swell with pride. Not too long ago, she popped her head into my office and proclaimed, "Mom, did you know I only have four more summers until it's time for me to go to college?" I think I stopped breathing. After regaining my composure, questions started to flood my mind. Have I equipped her to follow Jesus? Does she know how to create and sustain

Christian community? Did I recognize her gifting and help her shape it for God's glory?

Overwhelming stuff, right?

Upon reflection, I thought about all the ways God has equipped me to care for her and how He has been sufficient for both of us. What I mean to say is that God gave me a heart for discipling my children and, throughout the years, I have radically altered my life to accommodate this calling. I have lived this active-duty military life and my faith in God in front of my children—falling and failing through each and every step. Humbling myself, apologizing, and modeling faith in Jesus has been at the very center of it all. In other words, the whole journey has been perfectly imperfect. I have made mistakes, lost my cool, and failed forward, with my children watching the whole time. And that's just how I believe God intended it to be.

The Bible has something to say about the way we should parent our children. Even if you don't have children, don't skip this part. The missional nature of motherhood is not restricted to those of us who have children. The calling of spiritual mothering is alive and well. In my many years leading women, I know one thing for certain: women are always looking for someone to disciple them at every stage. We should all know what the Word says about the responsibility of parenting, whether those parents are directly connected through birth or adoption, or if the connection is a spiritual one. For me, I am beyond blessed by the women in my circle who have stepped up to the plate to offer guidance, wisdom, and the love of the Lord to my children in a maternal and nurturing way.

Deuteronomy 6:5–7 gives us an idea of what our commitment to Christ calls us to do in relationship to children. It reads,

> You shall love the LORD your God with all your heart and with all your soul and with all your might. And these words that I command you today shall be on your heart. You shall teach them diligently to your children, and shall talk of them when you sit in your house, and when you walk by the way, and when you lie down, and when you rise.

Essentially, this passage is teaching us that we should be living out our love of the Lord in everyday ways, in everything we do.

In this passage, Moses, who wrote the first five books of the Bible, is teaching God's people that we should be pursuing our relationship with God fiercely and consistently. We should be reading God's Word often enough to know what it says and act on it, keeping it close to the surface and on our minds. In addition, this passage is telling us to pass this wisdom to our families through a specific action: teaching.

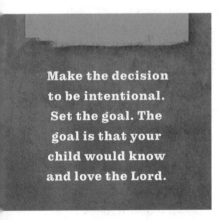

Make the decision to be intentional. Set the goal. The goal is that your child would know and love the Lord.

With the unending craziness of our lives—the moving, resettling, readjusting, and restarting—the task of raising disciples in this mess can feel impossible. But take courage. If you're reading this book, you are most likely already doing it.

MAKING IT WORK IN YOUR FAMILY

Here are a few pearls of wisdom and practical ways you can take on the task of discipling children toward loving the Lord.

First, make the decision to be intentional. Set the goal. The goal is that your child would know and love the Lord. The pathways and methodologies toward this goal may differ, but the motivation to get there is key. Sit down with your spouse and talk about ways to intentionally respond to the task of disciple making. Are there changes in your lives that need to be made? This scenario isn't the same for everyone, but for our family, we decided to pull our children from the public education system in order for me to disciple them through homeschooling for a season. As a Bible teacher, who better to raise up my children in the knowledge and worship of the Lord than me? Now, for the first time in four years, our children are venturing back into the public school sector as I follow God's calling to serve Him in ministry.

We also set boundaries around sports and our commitments to extracurriculars. We don't attend sporting events if they conflict with Sunday worship services or require us to run ourselves into the ground in the name of athleticism.

Now, don't get me wrong. I have nothing against extracurricular sports! In fact, on any given night of the week, you can find our family with hot dogs in hand at a baseball field. What I am saying is that we are not ruled by the current cultural expectation that families should live and die by the hustle of school schedules or sporting events.

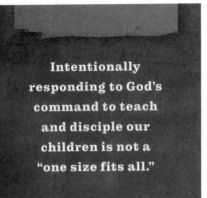

Intentionally responding to God's command to teach and disciple our children is not a "one size fits all."

When I think about the hours our children will be away from home this year, and comparing our experience in home-schooling, I know that I will have to be intentional with our time. Every moment counts, and I am learning (the hard way) that my husband and I have to be totally reliant on the Lord to help us. We are called to create an environment that fosters a love of God, an understanding of the gospel, and a realization that we, as a family, are called to live differently in response.

It's important to reiterate that this decision process, the process of intentionally responding to God's command to teach and disciple our children, is not a "one size fits all." You might have a discipleship time as a family or read books of the Bible together at night. You may be the main parent implementing these concepts if your spouse is away; or your spouse might not be a believer. The way this principle fleshes out really is different for every family. The key factor to consider is the response to the call itself. God is calling you to make the discipleship of your children a high priority. Becoming a follower of Jesus means "signing up" to lead your families.

Here's the encouraging part of this truth. We are supposed to do this task in our everyday routines, and nowhere in Deuteronomy did God say it had to be perfect. Late one night, my phone rang. A close friend, whose child attended a Christian preschool, was on the line. She was frantic because the school requested that each child bring a copy of their favorite children's Bible for an activity. Her son had a few favorite Bible storybooks, but because he was only three, she had not yet purchased a full-fledged Bible for him. The pressure she was putting on herself manifested in her voice and all I wanted to do was reach through the phone and give her a hug. In my own season as a young mom, I was obsessed with doing all the things right. I bought all the books, the Bible nursery rhymes, and stuck Bible story stickers all over the walls.

Nearly fourteen years later, I now know that, while all these things are nice, they aren't necessities. If I'm honest, all the books and curricula I bought required so much more effort than I had. I ended up putting them on a shelf somewhere and forgetting they existed. Instead, one of the most profitable things I have done is to live out my love for the Lord in practical ways in full view of my children. Worship music frequently plays in the background of our home. Many times, I can be found at my kitchen table, lost in a book of the Bible. My children are very familiar with the sight of multiple commentaries and reference books scattered all over our coffee table when Mom is in full hyperfocus mode. Additionally, for as long as my youngest has been alive, Thursday mornings have been spent on mission. Every week, our home is opened for small, local, and intimate Bible studies. Women gather together, huddled around our twelve-person table with Bibles in hand. All our children have watched us pray, study, cry, and support one another in Christian friendship. We have shown them, in our actions, that Christ is King and He is worthy of our worship. This real-time visual, an immersion in Christian fellowship, beats out any attempt a book or curriculum could produce.

WHEN YOU MESS IT UP

But before you hear me say "I've got it all together" or start to believe I had the patience of Job when I homeschooled, I'll set the record straight. "Patient" has never been a word I would use to describe myself, nor would it be the choice description of anyone who truly knows me. I'm hot-headed and an anxious ball of wax 99.9 percent of the time. Clutter drives me absolutely nuts and I operate in a gridlock of rigorous schedules and airtight time blocks. Just ask my children how fun-loving and carefree I am when plans change or schedules shift.

The second verse to the life song of loving Jesus in front of your kids is to humble yourself when you utterly mess it up. How this works out in your daily life, especially when you completely lose your ability to adult, is to fess up and ask for forgiveness. An honest, authentic apology is just as much your testimony to your kids as your ability to teach them about the gospel. You are going to fail and fail often. You will yell, get overwhelmed, and there will be guilt.

But don't believe the "mommy wine culture." You need Jesus more than eighteen cups of coffee or a five o'clock wine run. "Self-care" won't do the trick either. Don't think I'm saying that time to yourself is bad, or that setting aside time to prioritize your needs is not important. It most certainly is, but when we are talking about the work of discipling your children in your everyday life, the answer isn't "be the happiest you can be." The answer is to faithfully fall forward—to be the holiest you can be and trust God to do the rest.

BETTER TOGETHER

The last integral thing I've learned about missional motherhood over the years as a military mom is the importance of doing life together with other mothers. Let me tell you about my neighbor and coffee mate, Christina. She spent her entire teaching career as an early educator pouring into children, encouraging them, and raising them up for success. When she, too, fell in love with a military man, life took a vastly different turn. Now, as a military spouse, she is frequently on the move, and with a few little ones in tow, she set out on a new path. When I say she takes discipling her children to a whole other level, it is the understatement of the year. Her God-given gift of teaching and sharing God's truth with children seems to be at her very core.

In contrast, as a former homeschool mama of four, my sweet spot for teaching starts around sixth or seventh grade. I love literature, language, and logic. I struggled with the early education years, and finger painting my ABCs is not the most joyful point of my day. When I met Christina a few years ago, we had both just recently relocated to south Mississippi. Mutually connected through other milspouse friends, we decided to meet up for a coffee chat. This coffee chat grew into accountability and Bible study. Before I knew it, I was bawling my eyes out because the task of homeschooling my then six-year-old was too much. "I don't know how to teach her how to read!"

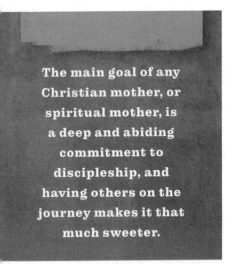

The main goal of any Christian mother, or spiritual mother, is a deep and abiding commitment to discipleship, and having others on the journey makes it that much sweeter.

I cried. "I'm doing this all wrong! She'll never be able to read and I'm completely failing her."

A light twinkled in my friend's eyes as she sprang up and said, "I would love for her to come over and do school with us a few days a week! That way, you could focus on your older kiddos, and she could play to learn." I cried again. Honestly, I had been begging God for encouragement in this area and was really longing for someone to help. After that fateful conversation, my youngest daughter started spending three mornings a week with our new family friend. Through her joyous attitude and passion for teaching the young, Christina has also sharpened my faith and blessed my soul. She gave some tips and tricks to work with my daughter at home and helped me come up with new ways to teach God's beautiful truths to my baby.

I can't tell you how important it is to find other women who are in the same mess of motherhood with you. They enrich this journey in ways that are difficult to describe. You will find women out there who are genuinely pursuing the Lord in amazing and wonderous ways. Their gifts are awe-inspiring, and they have the ability to encourage your faith as you seek to make disciples out of your children. Ultimately, walking in community with other mothers models our love for the Lord and our honest expressed need of encouragement. Our children are watching. They see the effort, the failures, and everything in between. By allowing other women to pour into us and our children, we are reinforcing an awesome truth. Motherhood is not easy, and we surely won't do it perfectly, but the main goal of any Christian mother, or spiritual mother, is a deep and abiding commitment to discipleship, and having others on the journey makes it that much sweeter.

Take a second this week to connect with another mom or join a local mom's group. Look for opportunities to set up play dates or, if you don't have your own children, check on a friend or family member with young kids. Here's the thing. You'll never know just how much impact you can have on the next generation just by showing up. Think back to when you were younger and ask yourself, *Would I want someone like me around to show me how to love the Lord*? I bet you would, and now you have the chance to stand in the gap for a generation of kids today. Who knows if we could ever even measure the impact or count the blessings given? Jesus has called us to this time, to this culture, and to follow Him by leaving a legacy of faith.

Your Turn

1. Describe the legacy you desire to leave for your children.

2. What steps can you take today to more intentionally focus on these goals?

3. Who is on the journey with you toward "a deep and abiding commitment to discipleship"?

PART TWO

Love People

Beloved, let us love one another, for love is from God, and whoever loves has been born of God and knows God. Anyone who does not love does not know God, because God is love. In this the love of God was made manifest among us, that God sent his only Son into the world, so that we might live through him. In this is love, not that we have loved God but that he loved us and sent his Son to be the propitiation for our sins. Beloved, if God so loved us, we also ought to love one another. (1 John 4:7–11)

Love. What does it mean to love? Can we create a working definition of love, or does God give us a clear picture of this concept? First John 4:7 reminds us, "Let us love one another, for love is from God, and whoever loves has been born of God and knows God." If we fast-forward to the next verse, we see "God is love." The Greek word used in this passage is *agape*, which translates into the phrase "take pleasure in" or "demonstrate love."[4] Love is more than just an emotion or acting upon an emotion. Love is a person. God is love. Love is also the mark of a follower of Christ. The culmination of God's law can be summed up in this: Love God and love one another. In the next few chapters, we are going to explore how loving others fleshes out in Christian military life.

4

We Signed Up to Be Part of a Local Church

The first Sunday after a fresh PCS is one of the hardest to get through.

Boxes line the hallways of an empty house. Grief and excitement fight for ruling the disposition of my heart. The anxiety of fast-paced packing and coordinating a cross-country move is at an all-time high. My body is weary. My mind is tired. All I want is a friend, a kind word, or someone to know me when I walk into church on Sunday morning. I want my friends, my church family. But now they are states away and I am preparing myself for some inevitable disappointment.

My favorite part of finding a new church home after settling down is that first, good church lady hug. You know the one I'm talking about—the hug you receive from the familiar woman who serves the coffee or holds the babies. This woman, whoever she is, recognizes you from across the room, knows your name, and remembers your children. She makes a beeline through crowded seats or a packed fellowship hall to envelop you in a much-needed embrace. This moment is more life-giving than words can describe.

The church is where we are meant to belong.

In 2014, our family relocated from Hamilton, Ohio, to Keesler AFB in south Mississippi on a sunny Friday afternoon. Our children were only two, four, and six. Our fourth child wasn't even an idea yet. We unloaded the semitruck we had just trekked down for a thirteen-hour drive and went out for supper as a family. The first thing we talked about over our shrimp dinner was finding a church to visit. We asked around online, on spouse's pages, and such. I researched a number of the local churches online, even listening to some of their sermon series. We finally landed on a church in the next city over.

"Is that Rilo Kiley playing in the background?" I asked Keith (shout-out to all my underground indie rock fans, circa 2003). We wandered into an open sanctuary full of stack-and-set seating (and some really great intro tunes). This church was an older church plant but operated in a mobile format, meaning that they met at a skating rink and set up and tore down each weekend service. The pulpit was constructed out of a makeshift stage with

PVC pipe holding up white fabric in the background. It was a no-fuss, no-muss type of place, seemingly stripped down to the bare essentials. I loved every minute of it. This place seemed like it hosted a group of people who really only cared about authentic relationship. We were home.

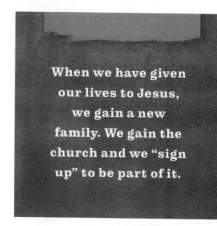

When we have given our lives to Jesus, we gain a new family. We gain the church and we "sign up" to be part of it.

Curious to see more, I walked my kiddos to the children's ministry rooms in the back. The children's ministry workers were amazing, even helping one of our screaming children adjust. Our then youngest son was always hesitant to be dropped off, so while we'd wait for him to acclimate every week, we were able to really get connected with Justin, the Family and Community pastor. Justin, who would become one of our closest family friends, made sure to plug our family in to the life of our new local church. He connected us with another group of military families who met weekly in the on-base housing neighborhood and encouraged us to get involved with the life of this local church, serving and participating in the ministries they offered.

This particular church did three things really well. First, the pastors, ministry leadership teams, and the congregation all made a big deal about the Bible. What I mean is the church took teaching the Scriptures seriously and, from the pulpit, the pastor preached line by line through books of the Bible. They valued expository preaching. Second, they really focused on living in community—on doing life together outside of the context of a Sunday worship service. Last, this church was committed to living missionally. Without this church and some of its leaders, I don't know if I would have ever learned to love the Word in the way I do today.

A PART OF THE FAMILY

When we have given our lives to Jesus, we gain a new family. We gain the church and we "sign up" to be part of it through serving and prioritizing the task of creating Christian community. The church is made up of people who have been saved, who have repented and put their trust in the risen Jesus. They have been baptized in faith and gather together to worship God, proclaim the gospel, disciple one another, serve their communities, and evangelize the lost. The church is a people. It is not an event, a building, or a singular denomination. The church is, and always will be, God's Plan A for carrying the redemptive story of Jesus to the four corners and we are called to participate.

First Corinthians 12:21–26 says,

> The eye cannot say to the hand, "I have no need of you," nor again the head to the feet, "I have no need of you." On the contrary, the parts of the body that seem to be weaker are indispensable, and on those parts of the body we think less

honorable we bestow the greater honor, and our unpresentable parts are treated with greater modesty, which our more presentable parts do not require. But God has so composed the body, giving greater honor to the part that lacked it, that there may be no division in the body, but that the members may have the same care for one another. If one member suffers, all suffer together; if one is honored, all rejoice together.

I'm guessing you can surmise that I really do love the apostle Paul and his letters to the New Testament church. Here he is again, talking about the nature of the church. He compares the church to a body. Just as our body is made up of all different parts, the church is made up of all different people. Each part, or person, is a functioning member, moving and participating, forming beautiful imagery of connectivity, unity, and oneness. In the church, there is also a very present theme of needing each other, being unable to dismiss one part or do without another. We all bring a vibrancy to the body of Christ, and learning to love people well begins here.

I can acknowledge the hardships of stepping up to do this hard work. Finding a new church home can be daunting. You may or may not have access to churches in your denomination. The churches near to you might still be a fair distance away from your installation. Or the churches around might not have a children's ministry or the programs you're looking for. Social anxiety, PTSD, or other hinderances may place obstacles in committing to a local church. However, there is so much value in striving toward committing to a local church. And it is a matter of obedience.

The book of Acts is one of my favorite books in the Bible. Why? Well, let's review a bit. There are three overarching narratives in the Bible. The first is the entire Old Testament, the story and history of God's people—who they were and what they did. Specifically, it is the recorded history of God's faithfulness to His people.

The second narrative is the four gospel accounts in the New Testament. These chapters outline Jesus' virgin birth, sinless life, sacrificial ministry, and miraculous resurrection.

The third narrative is the birth of the early church, described in Acts, and continued in the epistles. Jesus had promised the Holy Spirit in John 14, and in the beginning of Acts, before Christ ascends to heaven, He tells His disciples something amazing. In Acts 1:8, Jesus says, "You will receive power when the Holy Spirit has come upon you, and you will be my witnesses in Jerusalem and in all Judea and Samaria, and to the end of the earth." After He said this, Jesus ascended, and the church was born. The

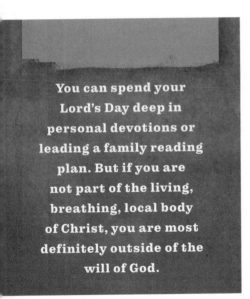

You can spend your Lord's Day deep in personal devotions or leading a family reading plan. But if you are not part of the living, breathing, local body of Christ, you are most definitely outside of the will of God.

church has a function—to be witnesses to the ends of the earth—and we have "signed up" to join the action. YES!

When we commit to a local church, to make the decision to attend, submit, and participate in a local body of believers, we obey God's calling to belong to His people and submit to Jesus' establishment of a public group of people who serve as witnesses. In this group, we affirm each other's faith in Christ, agree to the lifelong commitment of discipleship, and place ourselves under the leadership of elders and ministry leaders who help us be accountable to biblical living and belief.

Ultimately, being a member of a local church and being shepherded and cared for by leaders God has established is His design. You can watch all the online sermons taught by all the headline-making leaders and preachers, and still be spiritually starving. You can spend your Lord's Day deep in personal devotions or leading a family reading plan. But if you are not part of the living, breathing, local body of Christ, you are most definitely outside of the will of God. There is no such thing as a perfect church, nor is there any shortage of church-based scandals. But nevertheless, there is a church family God has specifically laid out for you, a place to be served and to serve. A place you belong.

IT'S WORTH LOOKING FOR

There are so many new things we are told to change or reprioritize when we place our faith in Jesus. At some level, we know the Bible has something to say about a topic and we should seek it out. We may know the importance of prayer, or even experience the urge to join a small group of sorts. We have a deep-seated longing to have a place where we are accepted and welcomed, but do we know what that longing means or where to start? The truth is that we should start with the church because this is where it is designed to start.

You may have a plethora of excuses to explain why church attendance is too much. "We are too busy" or "We aren't comfortable in new churches." I get it. The work of seeking out and joining a local church is positively overwhelming and can be really exhausting. Not to mention that you may be carrying some immense church hurt. But the cost is still worth it.

Maybe your last church was absolutely amazing, and now you don't even want to try to rebuild what you've lost. If so, know that I see you and I understand exactly how much I'm asking. I have built and rebuilt community within a local church more times that I can count. It is grueling work and comes with a steep emotional price tag. But I hope I can convince you that you are in desperate need of a lifeline—a direct connection to God's people—in order to flesh out your faith while living as an active-duty family. You cannot and should not do this life alone. The effort you will make toward tethering yourself and your family to a church is an act of worship.

It goes without saying that there will certainly be times where you are dissatisfied with your current circumstances, whether the church you want is nowhere near or the church you have falls drastically short of your expectations. Know this: the Lord works in and through both circumstances, and the product is a more resolved, resolute faith. God grows you through the local church, His Word, and the equipping of His Spirit for your good and His glory.

So, do the hard things. Make the space to try out and sit in with a local church this weekend. Don't wait. If you're still not sure how to go about the "church shopping" process, here are a few helpful tips. If you are preparing for a PCS or just looking for a fresh start, take some time to check out church websites and maybe watch a few sermons. Some of my favorite websites to start looking are 9marks.org, using their "church search" option, or thegospelcoalition.org/churches. Each of these websites showcase a myriad of local churches and might be a handy place to start looking, especially to find one that holds a high view of Scripture. In addition, I have a sort of checklist I use to filter our family church search.

Does this church value expository preaching?

Is the worship focused on the Lord?

What does the approach to build community look like in the church?

What role does mission and evangelism take in the church?

As a side note, I do place value on things like children's ministry and other programs designed for families. These ministry opportunities are wonderful and may be just what your family needs. These add to the experience of a local congregation, but they are not necessarily the first things I look for. The reason we, as believers, attend church is to come together for corporate worship and to hear the Word preached. Simultaneously, we are to care for each other—walking alongside one another and doing everyday life together. Also, how a church feels about missions and outreach says a lot about it. A church should encourage and equip its members to be sharing the gospel and making disciples. And a church that empowers missionaries to go where we can't to engage the lost is a treasure indeed.

Look for things that really matter and make impact when you start the venture of church hunting. I have no doubt there is a church family just waiting to invite you to the table and an open chair is there for you.

Your Turn

1. What do you look for in a church? What's important for your family?

2. Why is being part of a local church fellowship a necessary part of our commitment to Christ?

3. Have you hesitated to commit to a local church body? Why? What steps will you take to remedy this?

5

We Signed Up to Serve

I don't know what magical properties lie within a freshly glazed donut served with a hot cup of coffee, but I have to admit, whatever it is always does the trick.

When I find myself driving the struggle bus and stumbling through the doors of our local church on early Sunday mornings, these two items seem to melt my stress away and ready my heart for a time of worship. My children, who could be half-groomed and consumingly cranky, drag themselves to the counter where they know a nice lady would be waiting for them with a breakfast pastry in hand. The church coffee bar was, and still is, the first place our motley crew crashes in when we roll up on Sunday mornings. As a matter of fact, this humble corner was the first place I started to serve when our family finally felt at home in a Sunday service.

So *I* became the nice lady behind the counter with a hot cup of coffee in hand and donut in the other. I may or may not have eaten my fair share before my shift started, but nonetheless, I left plenty to hand out. This position, serving others, presented me with so many beautiful gifts. I learned names and faces. I welcomed newcomers and made fast friends. The other men and women behind this corner coffee shop also carried the burden of creating new connections. I found it was the gateway to really plugging in and participating in the ministry of the church at a deeper level. In working to serve, God used this sacrificial time to bless me abundantly and help me to tangibly follow Christ's example of love.

A TIME TO SERVE AND A TIME TO BE SERVED

I want to handle this next section with care because the last thing I want you to hear as you walk through the next few paragraphs is the command to do more than you are currently capable of doing. When I began serving at the church, my husband was stateside. Our children were relatively young but no longer nursing or clinging to my hip, so I did not have overly extravagant demands on my time. I had the mental and physical capacity to serve every other weekend or so at the coffee bar. Eventually, I moved from the coffee bar to holding babies. After that, I found my way into leading a discipleship group with my husband, Keith. Ultimately, I have to admit, I grew into a serial server, and I've loved nearly every minute of it.

A few years passed before God called us to help plant a new church. There, I served in multiple capacities, mainly women's ministry and community group leadership. It was one of the most beautiful seasons.

When our church plant was nearly a year and a half old, we PCS'd to a new station in Georgia. Before long, Keith was deployed and the capacity to serve left with him. I could barely crawl my way to church, much less arrive early to

> **Maybe now is not the time for grand gestures of servanthood in the church or huge time blocks of commitment. Maybe this season is the time for you to *be* served, filled up, cared for, and refreshed.**

hold babies or pour coffee. The everyday routine became even more complex when we began our school year. My mental, physical, and emotional real estate were completely filled up. Serving for long periods of time or committing to six-month-long positions were totally a "no-go." So, hear me say, sweet friend, "It's okay." It is okay if now is not the time or the place for grand gestures of servanthood in the church or huge time blocks of commitment. Maybe this season is the time for you to *be* served, filled up, cared for, and refreshed. If it is, communicate this truth to your church leadership when they ask if you can sing, serve, or sweetly rock babies. Just know, when you are ready, Jesus invites us to know and serve Him through caring for others well.

FILLING A GAP

What does it actually look like to serve others or be in a mindset of servanthood? Depending on where your church is geographically located and who attends the services, the ministries offered by any given local church can vary. Churches in more metropolitan areas may host food pantries or homeless initiatives. Churches near new developments and subdivisions may be more family-focused with larger children's or youth ministries. If the church is established and near a military installation, there might be some contextualized ministries for the military community. Any of these places would offer a multitude of options to serve. You might even come up with a new way to engage with the local and surrounding community through discovering a specific need that is not currently being met.

One of my favorite parts of serving is to take notice of the gaps in a new place. Every single station I've ever moved to had a specific need that went unmet. On reflection, I can look back at how God used every opportunity when I obeyed in serving, which increased my love for Him and for others. He grew my faith in ways I could not have experienced apart from serving, and He gave me the gift of new friendships in and through serving with fellow believers. Ultimately, Jesus sets the example of serving for us, instructing us that serving is a worthy endeavor, and the act of serving others is love in action.

As I've said, I was twenty years young when Keith and I were married, and in those days, we were stationed in a tiny town in northern Mississippi. One day, while poking through my closet, I found my senior prom dress shoved into the back of the rack. I fluffed it out a bit and held it up. Saving it for a military ball or formal event, I stuck it back in its place. Three years later, I had amassed a huge collection of formals and found myself expecting our second child. After a few graduation ceremonies, the Air Force Birthday Ball, and a handful of evening gown events, I had more than a couple of new dresses. My post-baby body convinced me I would never again see a single-digit sized garment, so I decided to clean out my closet.

Having only finished a few semesters of college, I freshly remembered high school and the specific hardships I faced as a teenager. I wasn't an overly girly girl (I'm still not), and there were a ton of underprivileged high schoolers in our local area. These dresses weren't going to do anything for me in the foreseeable future, but I wasn't sure about what to do with them. I called a few neighbors, asking them what they had done with all their outgrown gowns. We discovered each of us together had enough gently used dresses to donate them to at least fifty high school seniors.

Banding together, we built a volunteer project for the local military spouse community. The Cinderella Project was born.

We held fundraisers, leaned on the local spouse's club, and partnered with women in the local church. In total, by the end of the spring, we had collected over two thousand gently used gowns, and we hosted a free boutique right before prom season. Teen girls came all the way from the Mississippi Delta. Seamstresses volunteered to do on-site alterations, hair stylists came out for up-do tutorials, makeup artists showed up with complimentary samples, and a photographer even set up a backdrop to give the girls a free picture. Many of these women who served alongside me are still people I would call friends today. God used our efforts to serve these girls to draw me nearer to Himself and to give me a heart for youth-aged kids. I left Columbus, Mississippi, in my early twenties with a new passion and full heart from showing Christ's love and provision.

NOT AN OCCASION BUT A LIFESTYLE

At our next duty station, because of my newly discovered excitement around serving youth-aged kids, I volunteered to serve in the church's youth group. After a few years serving in youth group, I graduated to serving as a MOPS (Mothers of Preschoolers) coordinator. When all of my children were five and under, I began to see serving as an opportunity to use my hands while being able to connect with the other women in my church in meaningful ways. MOPS gave me a taste for women's ministry and a desire to grow my understanding of how to serve women well. Nearly ten years after organizing my first dress drive, I was on my way back to Mississippi for a new assignment, a new church family, and a handful of donuts.

First Peter 4:10 says, "As each has received a gift, use it to serve one another, as good stewards of God's varied grace." The Scripture goes on to describe two kinds of gifts: acts of speaking and acts of serving. Peter, a disciple of Christ and apostle in ministry, is teaching about the nature of "stewarding" the good gifts God gives in the church. We all have something more to bring to the table than filling a seat during Sunday service. And the church you're attending has so much more to offer you than an empty seat to sit in. We can find an abundance of ways to "serve one another" at various seasons in life—whether through speaking, serving coffee, holding babies, leading a study, or something entirely different—and yes, this is what we "signed up" for.

What I'm really saying is that serving is a way of life. It has a way of showing us what is missing and where God is moving. Caring for others and meeting tangible needs for them grows us spiritually and connects us to God's people in beautiful ways, but the bottom line is that serving is not self-motivated. Ultimately,

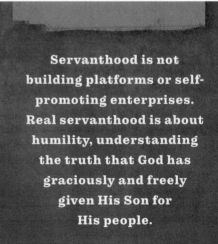

Servanthood is not building platforms or self-promoting enterprises. Real servanthood is about humility, understanding the truth that God has graciously and freely given His Son for His people.

following Christ's example of humble servanthood allows us to set aside self-interest, and the process produces a life that mirrors Jesus.

On the other hand, the world will tell you to pursue *purpose*, not service, at all costs. We hear a distinct and resounding call to find out what you like to do: do it for Jesus (or yourself), turn it into a dollar, or write a bazillion books like the women on big stages. But life is not about our side hustles or pursuing the projects that make us famous. Servanthood is not building platforms or self-promoting enterprises—even though much of today's contemporary Christian culture seems to promote this message.

Real servanthood is about humility, understanding the truth that God has graciously and freely given His Son for His people. In seeking the well-being of others, we get the privilege of experiencing God's love by giving it away to others.

TO SUM UP

You might check with your local church to see where the gaps are. Ask someone in leadership where they need a few extra hands. Maybe you're not in a season where service is possible, or you're not sure about what you could even bring to a church body.

Discovery and development are always a great idea when it comes to uncovering what gifts you possess or how you should utilize them. It might be helpful to find a spiritual gifts assessment test and see what result you find. Maybe you have a specific gift and are looking for an opportunity to use it. Are you a writer? Offer to curate the church newsletter. Are you a tech savvy person and love a good sound mix? Churches are always looking for people to serve in the sound booth. Do you love feeding folks? There is such a need for hospitality in today's church.

Hear me say this: you have gifts—that God intended to use for His glory and your good. Serving allows us to mold and mimic our lives after Jesus and it becomes a pipeline to a deeper connectivity with those you serve. Don't miss out on all that God has for you in serving alongside His people. Working in a posture of humility and seeking to meet the needs of others has profound effects, both for us and those we are caring for. Through serving, we get to experience the grace and mercy of the Lord. We get to be His hands and feet, offering kindness, care, and compassion in His name.

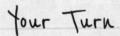

Your Turn

1. Why is service a part of the Christian life? In what ways are there times to both serve and to be served?

2. Where do you see a gap, or need, that you can help fill?

3. When have you enjoyed the pleasure of serving? What made the experience(s) meaningful?

6

We Signed Up to Live in Community

Two thirty in the morning is an extremely unconventional hour to be making chicken gnocchi soup, but that is exactly what we did.

None of us were getting any sleep on this particular night. A friend received some terribly difficult news and a flock of us met in the late hours of the evening to spend our time talking and encouraging her into the wee hours of the morning. At my kitchen table, in our humble military- issued abode, seven of us surrounded our friend in prayer. Holding hands and praying through tears, we asked God to be with us. We could feel that His presence was there to hold us all. I remember feeling overwhelmed in gratitude. I was grateful that my friend had a community to call and that I had the privilege of standing beside her, to stand together with a fierce throng of women who loved Jesus.

These women, from all walks of life, ages, and life stages, just seemed to be woven together. Our weird friend group had formed from a deep and desperate need for family. At the time, I was leading a ministry program in partnership with our local chapel. What started as a small group Bible study in my tiny box-shaped living room had grown into ten Bible studies that met simultaneously. As the Lord grew and multiplied our friendships, He grew and multiplied those we served. This before-daybreak soup crew was made up of study leaders, ministry volunteers, and a few other participants. We all loved each other dearly and wanted to support our friend as she waded through rough and choppy waters. We all were reaping the benefit of living in community.

If we fast-forwarded one short year later, three of us from this tight-knit crew would be circled up outside our local church, weeping and praying as we said "goodbye." Our family literally rolled out on a PCS from the church parking lot. Our small group of friends, which expanded to include our husbands and children, had become like a second family. These women were the sisters that I picked, and we love each other to this day with a supernatural level of compassion. We meet regularly, across states and oceans. We catch up over coffee through video chat almost daily. We know the ins and outs of daily life, we know when one of our kids is sick, and we know instinctively how to serve one another.

BUILDING COMMUNITY

Here's the thing to know. Community like this is built, not happened upon. What I mean to say is that this community didn't exactly fall into our laps. Each one of us had to work to weave every thread of trust and we labored long to be present for one another. We asked the tough questions, discovered boundaries, extended patience to one another, and carried each other's burdens. It has to be said that this work is not for the faint of heart. Our burdens are extremely heavy: PTSD and neurodivergence, trauma and heartache, oversharing and rejection sensitivity. Sounds fun, doesn't it?

In all honesty, walking alongside these women is one of my life's greatest joys and one of God's greatest gifts to me. They have taught me humility and empathy and have placed an immovable truth inside my heart. They have taught me to see the truth that I am fully seen and known, worthy of love, and accepted unconditionally by Jesus and those closest to me. We built this hearth of friendship, brick by brick, and with the encouragement and instruction held in Acts 2:42–47:

And they devoted themselves to the apostles' teaching and the fellowship, to the breaking of bread and the prayers. And awe came upon every soul, and many wonders and signs were being done through the apostles. And all who believed were together and had all things in common. And they were selling their possessions and belongings and distributing the proceeds to all, as any had need. And day by day, attending the temple together and breaking bread in their homes, they received their food with glad and generous hearts, praising God and having favor with all the people. And the Lord added to their number day by day those who were being saved.

The book of Acts is a recording of what the apostles did after the ascension of Jesus and the arrival of the Holy Spirit. The verses above speak to me in such an immense way and have served as a foundational Scripture in the life of our family. It was this passage that called my heart into full-time missions. Why? Well, this passage showed me that the Lord has perfectly positioned military community members and their families to serve as ambassadors for Christ. We, as military spouses, are master community builders and we have the capability to submit all of our challenges to God, watching Him redeem them.

The message in this text is compiling a description of the early believers, of the church. These people were devoted to the apostles' teaching. In other words, this people group elevated the importance of God's Word and took the time to know what He had to say. Early church members also valued fellowship—being in relationship with one another in Christ. The phrase "breaking of bread" refers to worshiping God through participating in the Lord's Supper, that is, corporate worship. Also, they committed to praying with and for one another.

To show their deeply held belief toward care and compassion, the text even says these people were selling things they owned to support and provide for other members in the group. By doing these things—studying Scripture, worshiping together, holding relationships with one another in Jesus, and praying together—they enjoyed great favor with the surrounding community and had "glad and generous hearts." What a blessing! But here is my favorite part. The last line in verse 47 says that this community resulted in pushing the gospel. People were being added daily to the ranks of the saved. Hallelujah!

Community is a blessing to each one of us *and* it is missional. I can't tell you how many relationships and connections have formed from the core three: the three of us who have stood by one another through long and lean times. Honestly, there have been seasons when it seemed we were taking turns walking through hellfire. But at the end of the day, we flocked to the church together, worshiping our Father. We sold our stuff, marketed, and leveraged our gifts to financially support our community. At one point, we were selling home-made Southwest egg rolls and cupcakes to fund adoptions, provide for foster care parents, help abused women in our community escape their situation and get to a safe place, and close the gap for families dealing with food insecurity. We would lose hours diving into the Bible and always found the ability to hold

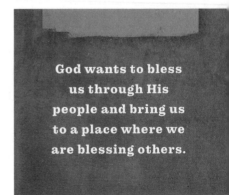

God wants to bless us through His people and bring us to a place where we are blessing others.

space for one another. This community is absolutely life-giving.

It goes without saying that seeking to live in community might be a discipline for you. All my introverted folks just gave a loud, collective gasp. "People-ing" is hard and sometimes the people inside the military can be a little crazy. Believe me. I know. I sometimes joke that, in addition to all the fun things swirling around in my head, I might legit have a case of "friendship PTSD." We all have that one friendship we thought would be fruitful go sideways. But the truth is God wants to grow you through this process and you're passing on the invitation. Life without Christian community is lacking. God wants to bless us through His people and bring us to a place where we are blessing others. We have to be committed to build a community that allows us to be served and creates the possibility for revival.

Community is only accomplished out of the overflow of a fulfilling and loving relationship with Christ and His church. We talked about plugging in and connecting through serving. Community building really is the overflow of these two things. When we plug in to a church and dive in through serving, we finish the groundwork for constructing a faith community.

Find out how your church helps in building a faith community. What does your church offer in community programs? Work within what they already have. Does the church offer a Sunday school group or a Bible study to kickstart connections in community? Is there a family ministry or lunch bunch? Start with one new family. It takes the intentional forming of new relationships. Ask someone new to meet for coffee or to join your family for a meal one evening. Perhaps your church does life groups or community meetups. Make the commitment to search for and build up a community that can catch your family and serve with you in tandem, and may the group be a blessing to everyone around you.

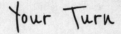

Your Turn

1. Who makes up your community? Or if community is something you're longing for, pray for it now.

2. How would life be different without community? In what ways is community a part of our commitment to Christ?

3. What opportunities do you have to expand your community? To serve out of community?

PART THREE

Live on Mission

I'll never forget the season when a young woman asked me what she needed to do to be baptized. This new military spouse had been attending our small group Bible study for a few weeks and was in the beginning stages of building her community. After sitting with the overarching story of Scripture, and really grasping the gospel, a fire in her heart was lit ablaze. "When can I get in the water?" she asked. We don't always get to see the fruit of ministry. But every once in a while, the Lord gives us the gift of watching a person come alive in Jesus and, for me, this was such a gift. I could hardly contain the joy I felt, knowing she would spend eternity with Jesus.

A few weeks later, with the first four rows of our home church filled with Bible study participants and their families, we all watched in awe as our sister emerged from the baptismal waters in a newness of life. As the pastor spoke the words and asked her the confirming questions of faith, I had the distinct pleasure of being a part of the ceremony. Immersing her in the water and pulling her back up, I couldn't tell where our tears ended and the baptismal waters began. One of many milestones in my own faith walk and in my journey as a leader, this moment remains at the center of my mind's eye when I think about what it means to live on mission—to make disciples.

7

We Signed Up to Be Radically Hospitable

A few years ago, our family left our beloved community at Keesler AFB for a brief stint in Warner Robins, Georgia.

Keith's time as an Instructor Supervisor had ended, and he was fanatically interested in a position with a mobile deployment unit. Because we were mandatory movers, we knew orders were inevitable and, when Keith applied for Georgia, we received approval in two days. Orders dropped. The house was packed. Before I knew it, our family trekked up the highway to our new home.

I dreaded the move. We had built such a life-giving community in south Mississippi. Our church home was flourishing, and

Keesler's local area had become the place where my heart for missions came alive. A part of me knew that the Gulf Coast was my heart's home forever. Watching the beach fade into a blur in the rearview mirror brought a tear or two. I grieved the loss. But as is typical, I'm pretty sure I wrapped all my emotions in Bubble Wrap and stuffed them somewhere with my dishes.

In preparing for our big move away from the land of sand and beach tacos, I had posted the obligatory spouse's page advertisement that read something like "For the love of Pete, will someone please talk to me. I need friends. Send help!" I think I also had been asking about local churches, Bible studies, and options for Christian fellowship. A woman named Pauline had engaged with my posts and reached out before we arrived in Warner Robins. She introduced herself over Facebook Messenger and suggested we meet for coffee after I got settled. The conversation continued and I discovered she served as the local homeschool co-op director for the curriculum we used. To encourage me, she swung by the base chapel on Robins AFB to snap a few photos of their ministry programs and service times. More often than not, as we messaged back and forth, she ended her messages to me with a heartwarming "Blessings to you today, sister."

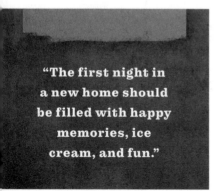

"The first night in a new home should be filled with happy memories, ice cream, and fun."

When we arrived at Robins AFB we were completely wiped out because the entire day had been fraught with calamity. As per usual with a military move, what's a PCS without a little insanity and crying kids? Thank goodness we decided to have the military movers take care of our relocation. I don't know if I could have handled doing that move ourselves. Days before, Pauline had texted me to ask about the time and day we scheduled our arrival and at the time, I thought nothing of it. It seemed like she was just making polite conversation. As it turned out, she'd hatched a bit of a scheme. Our truck pulled up to our house a little after lunchtime, and we spent most of the afternoon running around, getting groceries, and grabbing the last-minute essentials for a night on air mattresses. We ordered some Chinese takeout for supper, which we ate on folding tables and chairs.

Right after dinner, I received a message from Pauline letting me know she wanted to pop over for a second. She arrived at my front door with a thermal cooling bag full of a gallon of ice cream and some high-quality toppings: sea-salted caramel, dark chocolate, and fancy cherries. She had also purchased a brand-new board game, a game her family thoroughly enjoyed. She said, "The first night in a new home should be filled with happy memories, ice cream, and fun." I might have cried right then and there. Okay. I cried a lot. Her thoughtful gifts, and her intentionality in welcoming our family to a new place, settled deeply in my soul. From that day forward, I made up my mind to be as kind, thoughtful, and radically hospitable as she had shown herself to be.

"WHEN I WAS THIRSTY"

I try to hold a certain Scripture in the forefront of my thoughts most days. It's about a story in the gospel of Matthew, a place where we will be spending a little bit more time in these remaining chapters. The story takes place when Jesus is traveling, teaching and preaching about the kingdom of God. He encounters a lawyer whose intention is to trip Him up in His words. The lawyer asks, "Teacher, which is the greatest commandment in the Law?" Here is what Jesus had to say.

> "You shall love the Lord your God with all your heart and with all your soul and with all your mind. This is the great and first commandment. And a second is like it: You shall love your neighbor as yourself. On these two commandments depend all the Law and the Prophets." (Matthew 22:36–40)

Does this Scripture sound familiar? In an earlier chapter, we looked at the verse in Deuteronomy, which is worded very similarly. Love God. Love others. This may sound sort of elementary, but I can hardly help myself. I taught my children about the Ten Commandments (Exodus 20) this way. I had them hold up both of their hands. I instructed them to write "Love God" on their left hand and "Love others" on the right. I began, "We love God by obeying these commandments. We love no other gods, make no idols, revere the name of the Lord, keep the Sabbath holy, and honor our parents. We love others by honoring life, protecting our marriage vows, refraining from lying or stealing, and fostering an atmosphere of contentment." The theme continues as they write these commandments on each respective hand. It is a visual of "love God" and "love others."

God calls us to love Him, pursue Him, and worship Him with our lives. In addition to loving God with all we have, we are instructed to love others with the same ferocity. Jesus shows us, through His teaching and in His ministry on earth, how to love one another. In passage after passage in the gospel accounts of Matthew, Mark, Luke, and John, we see so many examples of how Jesus engaged with people. He served them with kindness and compassion, meeting tangible needs, and offering people real, authentic relationship.

A little later in Matthew, Jesus expounds on what it means to love people in practical ways. He is teaching the disciples about the kingdom of heaven and at the end of days, how He would sort those who actually followed Christ as King and separate those who did not. Let's look at Matthew 25:34–40.

> Then the King will say to those on his right, "Come, you who are blessed by my Father, inherit the kingdom prepared for you from the foundation of the world. For I was hungry and you gave me food, I was thirsty and you gave me drink, I was a stranger and you welcomed me, I was naked and you clothed me, I was sick and you visited me, I was in prison and you came to me." Then the righteous will answer him, saying, "Lord, when did we see you hungry and feed you, or thirsty and give you drink? And when did we see you a stranger and

welcome you, or naked and clothe you? And when did we see you sick or in prison and visit you?" And the King will answer them, "Truly, I say to you, as you did it to one of the least of these my brothers, you did it to me."

Hunger. Thirst. Welcoming. Provision. Sickness. Imprisonment. Look around at our active-duty and veteran military community. We are in abundance of those who are hungry. Active-duty families are experiencing food insecurity at alarming rates, and younger families are fighting to survive while living paycheck to paycheck. Even some of the more established men and women in the armed forces are struggling to put food on the table. Veterans sleep on the streets with heavy hearts and empty stomachs. Even if there isn't a lack of physical food and water for some, I guarantee that every single one of us has hungered and thirsted for friendship or community. We longed to be filled with acceptance or found ourselves with empty hands in a new place. There is hunger and thirsting here.

> Our community has long been imprisoned by loneliness, isolation, and exclusion. Most of us have, at one point or another, been stuck in this proverbial cell.

Also, when I think about all of the men and women who have bravely left their country of origin to start a new life with their new service member spouse in America, I am overrun with the conviction that we, as a community, should be actively pursuing friendship and connectivity with these people. They are sojourners—or visitors who are experiencing homesickness and culture shock. We should be radically welcoming and hospitable. Some of these practical exercises in love are pretty self-explanatory. There are people in our active-duty and veteran spaces who don't have access to basic living materials, such as clothing. We should be radically intentional to share what we have been blessed with, to provide aid. Our goal should be to serve those who are battling sickness and we should stand in the gap. Perhaps we could bring meals or watch children. There is no end to the list of possibilities of how we could serve a family who needs support through sickness.

What about imprisonment? Well, I can say from watching several of my sisters in Christ who serve inside prison ministries that they always need more people to walk alongside them, helping them reach and disciple men and women who have been imprisoned. But another thought I had, specifically related to our space, is this: Our community has long been imprisoned by loneliness, isolation, and exclusion. Most of us have, at one point or another, been stuck in this proverbial cell. What would it look like for us if we really observed the people around us and could identify whether or not they were locked up in feelings of loneliness? What did you want when you were alone in a dark room without comfort? For me, I know that all I wanted was a friend. When my spouse had boots on the ground somewhere else, and my children were very young, I longed for another adult. I longed for conversation that didn't revolve around snacks or toilet functions.

BE A FRIEND

What I am really trying to say is this: be a friend. Move and operate in a manner that communicates that you care. Observe your surroundings, taking notice of the people and places where kindness is lacking. Being radically hospitable is a calling that requires us to be awake, to be alert. We know the pain points of this military lifestyle. Among our peers, we have a uniquely shared suffering, a lifetime of sacrifices. We can enter into these spaces, no matter where we are, and speak for hope and encouragement with our actions.

In the next chapters, we are going to talk a lot about how living on mission fleshes out, but first, we start here. Ask God to make you more observant and to help you pay attention. Think about how you can personally step into spaces of hunger and thirst. Can you offer encouragement or provide needed items? Is there someone you can welcome in the name of the Lord? Ultimately, when you look around at all the things people are facing in their lives, do you ask the Lord to give you a loving heart and to show you how you can carry someone's burden with them? I'll end here with this truth.

In John 13:34–35, Jesus says, "A new command I give to you, that you love one another: just as I have loved you, you also are to love one another. By this all people will know that you are my disciples, if you have love for one another." Our love for one another marks us and identifies us as followers of Jesus Christ. When we started to follow Jesus, we "signed up" to love others well in His name.

Your Turn

1. When has someone shown hospitality to you?

2. What did Jesus mean when He said, "Whatever you do for others, you do for Me"?

3. What needs do you see when you look around? Which of these can you respond to, and how?

8

We Signed up to Open Our Homes

Thursday morning Bible studies have been a staple in my home for nearly eight years.

When our family first made camp at Keesler in mid-2014, we decided our south Mississippi home would be the headquarters for everything: fun, fellowship, and following Jesus. We wanted our home to be a place of welcoming, refreshment, restoration, and an open door for those who were looking for answers. Out of the overflow of the attitude of radical hospitality is the reality of an open door.

After a terrifying experience during a deployment at our previous duty station and the long-standing experience of feeling left out of local community, Keith and I felt compelled to use our four walls and a roof for ministry. In early 2013, Keith was sent to Afghanistan when our kids were five, three, and one. While he was tasked to deploy for an administrative detail, he ended up driving convoys and completed over a hundred missions outside of the wire in enemy territory.

A TURNING POINT

I was in my late twenties, and I thought I would be able to withstand the massive winds and waves of our first experience with deployment. I didn't know it at the time, but looking back, I had crippling postpartum depression. My weight yo-yoed up and down. Many days, I barely changed my shirt, much less showered. I couldn't figure out why I felt like such a failure, and every day was a race to survive until bedtime. When the kids finally went to sleep in the evenings, I practically melted into the floor. Getting up in the morning always started with tears and an unavoidable feeling of dread.

One such morning, with laundry and toys strewn all over the living room, I heard the doorbell. A postal worker stood outside holding a clipboard, and I could see my husband's footlocker peeking out of the back of her truck. She looked excited and made an upbeat comment about our soon-to-be homecoming. But Keith wasn't due back for months. You can imagine that at this point, I was completely undone, and my mind ventured into the worst of territories. I truly believed this postal worker beat the casualty officers to my door, as we were stationed remotely about an hour from the nearest installation.

As it turned out, Keith was totally fine. He had simply been transferred to a new location, and his belongings couldn't fit on the truck. So his stuff was shipped home before he could connect with me to let me know. But for three long and excruciating days, I lost hours staring at a blank wall and crying. At every turn,

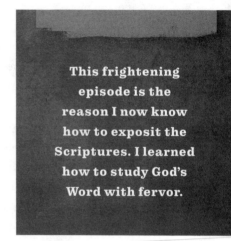

This frightening episode is the reason I now know how to exposit the Scriptures. I learned how to study God's Word with fervor.

I was reminded that I was alone and facing the scariest thing I had ever experienced. The tough truth was that there was no one to call and no one was coming. In a civilian community, I felt like a foreigner—a sojourner without a tribe. The feelings I carried crushed me. I still think those were the longest seventy-two hours of my adult life and let's be honest, the stress didn't help my depression.

As a Christian, I professed to believe in Jesus. But during this three-day endurance test, I discovered that I didn't know how to access this faith I claimed to have. Yes, I owned a Bible. But I had no idea what it said. Ultimately, in those silent and lonely hours, the Lord met me in that place and showed me what it really meant to pray without ceasing. He brought me to a place where reading His Word began to be a daily encounter. I dug deeply in the Word, found a new joy in getting healthy, and eventually overcame my postpartum depression.

This frightening episode is the reason I now know how to exposit the Scriptures. I learned how to study God's Word with fervor. Honestly, I can trace the beginnings of ministry to this very moment. If someone would have asked me ten years ago if this is where ministry for me began, I'm not sure I would have known how to answer. But now, after years of leaving the front door open and inviting military community members to our kitchen table, I can most certainly say that this earth-shaking season is when the Lord placed ideas about serving into the halls of my heart. My calling in ministry met firmly at the intersection of my greatest pain and my greatest pining, a longing I couldn't articulate with words.

I needed a friend who could understand. I remember begging God for comfort. What a difference a wiser and more seasoned military spouse would have made in that moment.

When our family relocated to Keesler in 2014, the first thing I decided to do was invite a few neighbors over for coffee and Bible study. I did not want even one more military spouse to experience such jarring things without a friend in Jesus or a companion to sit with in a time of need.

WELCOMING AND BEING WELCOMED

All throughout Scripture, we see God's people gathering together for worship, teaching, fellowship, and prayer. We find a common theme, a thread if you will, from the Old Testament to the New. This thread represents the idea that hospitality—specifically welcoming others to our hearth and homes—is a constant heart stance in God's people. In the Old Testament, God's law teaches about treating visitors, or foreigners, as natives (e.g., Leviticus 19:34) and loving them as you love yourself. Sound familiar? The prophet Isaiah teaches us concepts of sharing and bringing the homeless into our house (Isaiah 58:7).

During Job's suffering, he pointed out to the Lord that he had not allowed the sojourner to lodge "in the street," but that he had opened his "doors to the traveler" (Job 31:32).

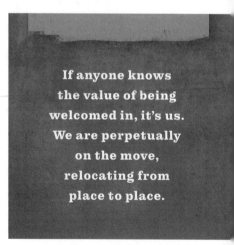

If anyone knows the value of being welcomed in, it's us. We are perpetually on the move, relocating from place to place.

In the New Testament, we often read about these same themes of showing hospitality and welcoming others. Examples are Romans 12:13, 1 Timothy 5:10, Titus 1:8, 1 Peter 4:9, Hebrews 13:1–2, and others. The point, of course, is that we should be hospitable, pursue a welcoming attitude, and open our homes.

If anyone knows the value of being welcomed in, it's us. We are perpetually on the move, relocating from place to place. The isolating feeling of an empty home after a fresh PCS is such a painful reminder that we must begin again in a place we don't yet belong. Our heart stance should humbly reflect our empathy for those who are constantly unwelcomed. When we foster hospitality in opening our homes, we pursue the heart of God. We are able to use our dwelling places for His work and His glory. The result is something immeasurably beautiful.

A SMALL START WITH BIG REVIVAL

On the very first Thursday morning Bible study meeting I hosted in my home, my newly befriended neighbor and I invited four more women in our community to come. One was a military spouse who had just married, and she was barely over eighteen. Another woman had a husband higher in the ranks and found herself an empty nester. Another participant was a career woman with "Dr." in front of her name. The final addition to our motley crew had two toddler children and no small amount of need for connection. This was us. We were a strange and straggly gathering.

Because we all resided in very different age groups, life stages, and lived experiences, the only thing I knew to do was to read straight from the Scripture. We walked line by line through the gospel of Luke. Before I knew it, our humble six had grown into seventeen. Less than a few weeks later, our numbers had grown to twenty-five. On one particular Thursday morning, I peered out the front window to see several women dragging lawn chairs and red wagons full of children down the street because they wanted to know what the Bible was all about. Eventually, we partnered with our local base chapel, opening a program with around forty women and nearly fifty children.

What started as one Bible study of six grew to ten Bible studies: ten leaders leading ten women each. By the time we outgrew the government staff, the facility, and the funding, the group had grown to over two hundred women and children. At this point in our ministry journey, we began teaching women how to open their homes and host studies in their own living rooms. Now, nearly ten years later, I'm not sure I could count how many Bible studies have multiplied out of the original group. I do know that there are groups meeting all over the globe; groups are in Japan, South Korea, Germany, England, Hawaii, and all over the Lower 48.

The decision to open our home so many years ago and use our living room as an extension area of the mission of the church changed the trajectory of the rest of my life. My life's work now consists of inviting military spouses to surrender to the gospel and the gift of salvation Jesus offers, to grow them in grace through the local church, and then to commission them out to make disciples.

JUST DOING IT

Approaching the task of creating an attitude of hospitality, specifically opening our homes to others in practical ways, looks like this. First, we ask God in prayer to show us the hurting in our community. Whether you live in military housing, off installation, or in an apartment somewhere, there are hurting people in your midst. Ask God to help you meet these people and to prepare your heart to receive them.

Second, prepare your home. I have to specify that I don't mean run up an enormous bill at your local home decor store. Nor do I mean to overspend on fancy furniture or create an atmosphere that will leave others envious or uncomfortable. Preparing your home means to identify places made for conversation and make them comfortable. The kitchen table is where I teach my Bible study. It's plain, but functional. I have enough chairs, plenty of paper coffee cups, and space for twelve to fifteen people.

Finally, get into the habit of inviting others over casually. While I do pick up before company, I have found that the laundry draped across the couch gives a nice pop of color in the living room. Don't worry about the clutter of everyday life or the assortment of toys on the floor. Invite women in anyway. Grab a coffee, host a play date, invite the neighbors for a taco bar. You can get creative, but the real heart of the matter is simply to open the door. You never know how impactful an invitation can be for someone in our space. Pray. Prepare. Invite people in.

Your Turn

1. When have you wanted and needed someone to open her home to you?

2. What are some memorable times when you've opened your home to others?

3. In what other ways can you make your home open to others? For a Bible study? A meal? Sharing childcare?

9

We Signed Up to Make Disciples

When I think back over the course of the last few years, I have to pause and reflect on the relationships God has given me.

The Lord has abundantly gifted me in His blessings through my husband—a man who introduced me to the saving and redeeming love of Jesus—and I've been sanctified and encouraged through my children. But there is one relationship that, when it comes to discipleship, takes the proverbial cake. Katie, one of my most beloved friends, has walked every step of this journey of disciple making with me. In fact, without her, my own story would look vastly different, and I truly believe I would not have ended up here . . . loving and leading women toward their Savior.

Growing up, I was never much of a girly girl. Making friends in my younger years challenged me. I've always been a bit of a loner and one of the most amazingly awkward people. I've struggled with inattentiveness, impulsive and excessive talking, and containing the explosive energy that pulses through my very being. To put it mildly, I am a completely excitable creature.

But from the time I was teenager, I learned to mask these features. I stored up "safe" responses in my head for when I entered into conversations so I wouldn't seem stupid. I mimicked the tone, cadence, and mannerisms of whoever I was speaking with, trying very hard to look like I understood what they were saying. Additionally, I have always been painfully self-aware and intuitive enough to realize the truth when someone I was around really didn't like me. Rejection sensitivity didn't (and still doesn't) do me any favors. I became anxious, fidgety, and aloof.

All the while, I focused intensely on my appearance: cutting my hair in a certain way, wearing the right clothes, and desperately trying to control how people saw me. An obsessive need for perfection drove my every move. Ultimately, a close and intimate friendship was something I believed was unattainable because I knew I could never bring myself to a vulnerable enough space for someone to truly know me.

THE REAL DEAL

It wasn't until I met Katie Byrd that the Lord began to show me the real meaning of friendship. I can trace His handwriting all the way back to the beginning. Looking back, it seems that He had woven our souls together in every single moment.

You know, some of the things I thank God for are a little silly. When I start to enter into praise and worship, every once in a while, a funny thought pops into my head and I have to thank Him for Dairy Queen, costume fairy wings, and the Applebee's fajita rollup. I know. Strange. But when we first moved to the Gulf Coast in 2014, our home in the military housing neighborhood stood on the outer edge of a cul-de-sac. Our "across the street" neighbors had a younger daughter about age five. My daughter, too, was five and finishing her first year of kindergarten. Since we arrived in April, the end of the school year wasn't far off.

One day, only two weeks after we unpacked, while my daughter and the neighborhood kiddos played in the nooks of our street, I met another mama. Katie. She had dropped by my neighbor's house to treat all the children with a trip to Dairy Queen because report cards had just been dropped. Before she pulled up, all the girls were swirling around our front yard. I remembered I had recently unpacked an entire box of fairy wings, tiaras, and ribbon wands that were left over from a birthday party. I gave each girl a new costume and off they flew. Katie came over to return the goodies and we stood there talking for a few moments. Mostly because I didn't want all the party supplies to come back into the

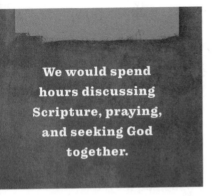

We would spend hours discussing Scripture, praying, and seeking God together.

house, I insisted she keep them.

Two weeks later, the church we had been attending hosted its annual Vacation Bible School. My neighbor and I decided to take our kids, if for nothing else than to get five minutes of quiet. Katie and her daughters were also already planning on attending VBS, so, after dropping off the kids, we all decided to head to the Applebee's around the corner from the church for dinner.

For the next three hours, I listened while Katie shared her entire life's story—trauma, hardship, struggles, and heartache. She gave voice to her doubts and shame, unloading a lifetime of sorrow and intimate details. Honestly, I found myself a little overwhelmed and no small amount of uncomfortable. I was always so guarded that the idea of sharing any of the stories she had dumped out on the table that night would have made me puke.

But every day for a week, we met for dinner and discussion, entering into each other's pain. The week after that, Katie and I lovingly refer to what happened next as the unending coffee hour. With a Bible in her hand, she started showing up at my house after elementary school drop-off, and we would lose hours discussing Scripture, praying, and seeking God together. Before we knew it, the time for school pickup and the bus runs had arrived.

During that season, I was consumed with denial and pretentiousness. I kept my home immaculate, frantically cleaning and staging every aspect of my life to look like I was doing okay, like I had everything together. On the inside, my emotions were a tumultuous mess, and I was terrified that anyone who really saw how I was feeling would immediately recognize me as an impostor. Simultaneously, Katie wore her trauma on her sleeve. She unabashedly shared encouragement and offered hope at every turn. Both of us were longing for the Lord, not always knowing how to get to Him.

Not too long into our endless coffee chats, we scrolled across a post on our local spouse's Facebook page. A military spouse in the next neighborhood over was leading a Bible study and inviting others to join. Katie and I bought our copies of *Calm My Anxious Heart* by Linda Dillow and decided to attend together. Jessica, only a few years older than we were, had a stunningly beautiful home. With four children, and two of them twins, I remember the first thing I noticed was that she was brave enough to have a white, upholstered couch. Every inch of her home welcomed us in. Fresh coffee brewed in the pot, and she had made some sort of fresh muffins. For the next six weeks, we sifted and savored the Scriptures together and unpacked our book. Neither Katie nor I had never been in a women's Bible study before, and we knew this group was the start of something amazing.

For the first two years of our friendship, Katie and I ravenously consumed Bible studies. Almost frantically, we would begin and complete six-to-eight-week workbooks in days. The local Christian bookstore knew our names and faces, as we were there once a week to purchase our next book or DVD set. I had been discipled by Jessica, a more mature believer, while also walking in a peer-to-peer discipleship relationship with Katie. All I knew was how phenomenal it felt for someone to share the knowledge and the wisdom of the Lord with me. Eventually, I followed Jessica's example. I opened my own home toward the task of disciple making. Katie, to this day, has attended every single one.

Throughout the last several years together, Katie and I experienced immense growth in our understanding of Scripture, found maturity in the faith, and have built a community together that reflects the mission and purpose of Jesus.

GOING DEEPER

In Matthew 28:18–20, Jesus says, "All authority in heaven and on earth has been given to me. Go therefore and make disciples of all nations, baptizing them in the name of the Father and of the Son and of the Holy Spirit, teaching them to observe all that I have commanded you. And behold, I am with you always, to the end of the age."

This passage is called the Great Commission. Jesus is speaking to His disciples, commissioning them to a very specific task. "Go and make disciples" is the core of this passage. What is a disciple? According to the *Moody Bible Commentary*, a disciple is "a follower, a pupil, an apprentice of Jesus," and being one includes "doing what He teaches and furthering His cause."[5] Jesus is telling us that all authority on heaven and earth belong to Him, and in this authority, we are to share a specific message, which accomplishes disciple making. The gospel is this message: the truth that Jesus died for the sin of God's people, that He was buried, and that He rose again. Because of Christ's finished work on the cross, you and I are offered grace upon grace. God, showing mercy, now looks upon us through the lens of Jesus' sacrifice. We are forgiven. Renewed. Free.

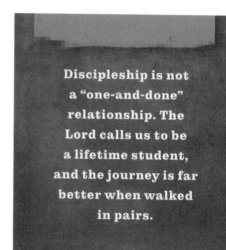

Discipleship is not a "one-and-done" relationship. The Lord calls us to be a lifetime student, and the journey is far better when walked in pairs.

The first question is this. Are you a disciple? When you look through the halls of your history, is the faith that you carry your own? Or is it a secondhand gift? Like a family heirloom, have you been dragging labels or Christian vocabulary through your life that has left you wanting more? If so, your very first step is to be still and take an honest look at Jesus. Ask God to reveal to you the beauty of the cross and the freedom only found in His Son. Find another believer, whether she is in your church or in your sphere of influence. Ask her for guidance and encouragement. Sit underneath the sound teaching of a pastor or ministry leader you trust. Dive into the Word, specifically one of the Gospels to get you started. There are four—Matthew, Mark, Luke, or

John. (Luke is a personal favorite. You can check out *Unexplainable Jesus* by Erica Wiggenhorn.[6])

If you are a disciple of Christ, my encouragement to you is to begin looking for the people that the Lord has brought into your life for the purpose of discipleship. Discipleship is not a "one-and-done" relationship. What I mean is that the Lord calls us to be lifetime students—to go deeper—and the journey is far better when walked in pairs. Perhaps there is someone in your friend group, your workspace, or even in your home, who requires you to be a disciple maker. Take a moment and ask God to show you who He is calling you to pursue in His name.

There is a passage in Acts 8 that I have camped out in for years. Really, the whole book of Acts is close to my heart. But the meat and potatoes of this Bible book outlines the birth of the early church and what the Holy Spirit accomplished through the apostles. In Acts 8:26–40, the author records an interaction between Philip, a disciple of Christ, and an Ethiopian eunuch. This eunuch, a high official in the court of Queen Candace of Ethiopia, was riding in his chariot and reading from the prophet Isaiah. Upon hearing a directive from the Spirit, Philip runs toward the chariot to speak with the man. Explaining the prophecy to the eunuch, Philip makes clear who Jesus is and what He has done. The eunuch believes, is baptized, and takes the gospel back to his motherland.

While I am paraphrasing, and really capturing this passage at a 50,000-foot view, I notice something convicting in the story. Philip ran. Now, back in biblical days, running would have been . . . undignified. They didn't wear "Hanes his-way," if you catch my drift.

Men did not run unless it was absolutely necessary. Before I get too carried away on the description here, the important thing to note is that he had such a sense of urgency to follow the Lord's leading in disciple making that Philip abandoned all else and charged forward. What about us? Who are we running toward with the gospel, without considering how we will look or sound? Are we willing to be obedient in following through with who God has called us to reach? The order is not small. We know from the Scripture in Matthew that God wants us to make disciples of "the nations." That means everywhere—in our

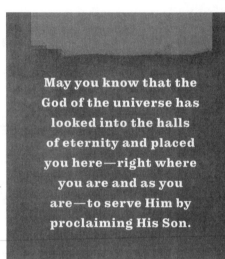

May you know that the God of the universe has looked into the halls of eternity and placed you here—right where you are and as you are—to serve Him by proclaiming His Son.

neighborhoods, school systems, circles of influence, cities, states, country, and abroad. Everywhere.

Maybe you're saying, "Okay, Megan. That's great. I have no idea how to even begin to do this." Take a deep breath with me and let's unpack. First, acknowledge the Lord. He gives us the obedience to follow through. It's His will for us to open the door, welcome women in, and serve them in lovingkindness. Our passage in Matthew also tells us about how we make disciples: teaching and baptizing. We are to teach the truths held in God's Word and follow the Lord's example in baptism. You cannot do it on your own. Ask God for the will to obey, the strength to complete the task, and for the conviction to believe disciple making is a noble endeavor. Stay strong in the faith. Let others encourage you. A great place to start is within the walls of the local church. Talk to your pastors or ministry leaders about the discipleship opportunities right where you are. Is there a ministry program or community group you can plug in to? Or is there a specific discipleship class or training they offer? There are so many resources out there for us to search and sift through.

Let's read through this passage again.

"All authority in heaven and on earth has been given to me. Go, therefore and make disciples of all nations, baptizing them in the name of the Father and of the Son and of the Holy Spirit, teaching them to observe all that I have commanded you. And behold, I am with you always, to the end of the age." (Matthew 28:18–20)

I love that this Scripture is the very last thing Matthew records for his audience. "And behold, I am with you always, to the end of the age." Jesus is with us, calling us to radically recalibrate our lives around His mission and His purpose. May we make disciples, through love and sound doctrine.

May you know that the God of the universe has looked into the halls of eternity and placed you here—right where you are and as you are—to serve Him by proclaiming His Son. May we finish this race, knowing what we signed up for, with grace and favor.

Your Turn

1. In what ways do you need to move past feelings of insufficiency to share Christ?

2. Who have you been discipled by at various times in your Christian walk? How are you involved in discipling someone?

3. Where has God placed you today? How can you "serve Him by proclaiming His Son" in this time and place?

Wrapping Up

To say this book was written during one of the most intense seasons of military life would be an understatement. When I started edging out the content in these pages, my husband was just returning from a one-year short tour in South Korea. Right before he was scheduled to return home, he had a terribly unfortunate accident, which caused his neck and shoulder to sustain heavy injuries. Our homecoming wasn't the one we'd planned for. Chronic pain and migraines definitely added to the stress of reintegrating two lives, budgets, schedules, and parenting types back into one lane. There were parts of this process when I almost admitted defeat, when I'd call a friend or two in tears. I wondered how well I would be able to communicate the form and function of disciple making when I felt like I was drowning.

All the while, I fixed my eyes upon the Lord, remembering the joy of my salvation. Jesus has been the rock that I have clung to in the storms of this active-duty military lifestyle. And I have dedicated my adult life to proclaiming Him to all who have ears to hear. Even during the lowest points of our family's journey through back-to-back deployments, a global pandemic, four hurricanes, and all other kinds of mayhem, I have longed to share the only source of hope I have.

God does beautiful things in and through our weakest spots.

Admittedly, the presentation or the word painting has not been perfect. Often, the Thursday morning Bible study found me tired and ragged. Showers were optional and let's just say, there were meetings that were not as smooth as they could have been. Here's what I'm getting at. Sometimes, when we look at our very poor and pitiful offerings for the Lord, we get discouraged. But what I have learned is that God does beautiful things in and through our weakest spots. I believe it is in this truth that we are able to release perfection, or even the pursuit of it. We can know, wholeheartedly, that God is in control and covering it all. He makes up the difference. He doesn't call us to be perfect, nor does He ask us to be a polished and pretty version of ourselves. He simply asks us to be faithful. He calls us to be faithful to Him and the things He calls us to do.

As a military spouse, we are perfectly positioned to serve God on mission. We already live our lives circled around a mission: to serve and stand beside our spouse, who serves and sacrifices for our country. We move every two to four years. We are master community builders. We are infinitely compassionate when it comes to welcoming newcomers. What if we took all the challenges and obstacles of this life—the high operations tempo, the moving, and the readjusting—and submitted them over to the Lord? What could He do in and through us if we would simply submit to the call of disciple making?

I believe, down in the very marrow of my bones, that the Third Great Awakening—that is, a revival unseen in the generation—will come from our community. We have the potential to release the largest mobilized and missional force this country has ever seen if we would just hold fast to the gospel and give it away fiercely.

God is raising up a fighting force within a fighting force to make immeasurable kingdom impact. Will you "sign up" for this?

A Letter from Megan

Dear Friend,

If you found yourself scrambling through the final pages of this book to find this letter, I see you. I wish we were sitting face-to-face and that I could hold the space to share this particular burden with you in person. I would sit across from you while holding your hand, and my greatest hope would be to impart some desperately needed encouragement. Over the years, as a women's ministry leader in military spaces, I have encountered more women than I wish to count who have been exasperated with the fact that their spouse does not submit to a holy God. They grapple with the balancing act of loving the Lord with the hardship of connecting with a spouse who does not value a deep and abiding relationship with the Creator of the universe.

Often, this circumstance brings about harsh feelings because partners in marriage struggle to maintain intimacy. Setting goals for their families, or even agreeing on how to accomplish them, is an obstacle. Church attendance may or may not be a high priority. Christian community may feel more difficult to construct. Parenting and problem-solving present a challenge because of a lack of unity. Arguments are not centered with biblical principles and, therefore, cause an inordinate amount of pain, bitterness, or resentment. The list can continue on, but here is the truth.

Find encouragement in this fact first: God is faithful, near, and in complete control of all our circumstances. He is present in all difficulties, and the hardships we endure are not useless. Romans 8:28 tells us, "And we know that for those who love God all things work together for good, for those who are called according to his purpose." What this means is that God is constantly working out His purposes for your life in and through the things that happen to you, the actions you choose, and the pathways you walk. God can and will use all things when we bring them to Him in prayer and surrender. Surrender is the act of forfeiting the results and outcomes of a particular scenario over to God, trusting Him and allowing Him to show where He has been working all along.

Second, your developing faith has influence and real-time impact on those closest to you. When you are wholeheartedly pursuing God, those around you will begin to notice changes in your attitudes, behaviors, and even in your thoughts. You are in the process of being made more like Christ; this is the process of sanctification. Jesus is the most compassionate, most loving, most selfless person in human history, and the nations are drawn to Him through His love. This love lives in you when you are fully submitted to Him.

There was a time when I was a militant atheist. I believed God to be a myth and worth no more than a single thought of denial. My husband is a cradle-to-the-grave believer, and his faith drew me nearer to my Savior. I don't say this to make a guarantee that your faith or trust in God will ultimately give you the same outcome. I certainly want you to hear that whether or not your spouse comes to the Lord, their belief in Christ or lack thereof does not depend entirely on the amount of faith you possess. Your spouse's response to the gospel is not your personal responsibility. Your role is to love the Lord, love those around you, and pray fervently for God to reveal Himself personally to your spouse.

Last, I want you to know that you are not alone, and you are not without resources. You can seek the guidance of your local pastor, Christian military chaplains, biblical counselors, or lay ministries for encouragement and wise counsel surrounding how to engage with a wayward spouse.

In much of my ministry history in the military community, I've also seen my fair share of marriages that were on unsteady ground because of a harmful spouse. *Do not hear this mandate of biblical marriage as a command to stay put in a hurtful or harmful relationship.* If you are experiencing physical, emotional, financial, mental, or sexual abuse at the hands of your spouse, I would instruct you to *get safe and seek wise counsel.*

Wise counsel should be sought by finding a licensed, clinical professional, preferably a Christian social worker or licensed Christian counselor. There is a distinction between a "biblical counselor," who does not require licensure or higher education, and a Christian counselor, who has acquired a higher level of education in a collegiate setting and has been required to complete state licensing standards. Typically, a biblical counselor is a layperson who voluntarily serves in and through the local church. They go through training and possibly earn a certification, but the standards are not always consistent, and this person may or may not be fully equipped to give wise counsel in the area of more difficult marriage dynamics, trauma, or abuse. Likewise, military chaplains might not always be your best option either. The best place to find professional help in cases of abuse is with a certified and trained clinician who holds not only to the sufficiency of Scripture and the knowledge held there, but also has a fundamental understanding of psychology and healthy relationships. With this person in your corner, you can discern and decide your next steps in healing.

I hope you hear my heart for you. I ache with you in the tension of your current circumstances and am praying for your spouse. I hope that you will continue to fiercely seek the Lord and that He may offer you comfort and courage as you face the days to come. May your spirit be full of grace, mercy, and confidence as you engage with your partner. May the Lord of hosts strengthen you in tangible ways, helping you to communicate truth clearly, love fully, and lead your family in mercy.

In Him,

Megan

Acknowledgments

This book is meant to be a love letter to the younger, more unaware version of myself and all of those like me. As a new military spouse, I had no idea what kind of life I was getting into, nor is it lost on me that I am still counting the cost of military service. But creating a resource like this for future generations didn't happen without a host of amazing individuals and communities who are such an integral part of my own journey.

To each of you, I am beyond grateful for your investment into my life as a military spouse and mother. Even more so, the mission work I am privileged to do is in no small part due to your kindness, instruction, and encouragement. To God be the glory and my deepest thanks to you.

To the Fam: Keith, for all the takeout, tiny tantrums, and midnight writing raids I've done over the past season . . . Thank you for making the space and loving me well. To my children: Hannah, may you always know that God has perfectly positioned you to serve Him in love. Beau, your heart and compassion for others encourages me daily. Noah, I pray your enthusiasm for life never dwindles and you fiercely pursue God's calling on your life. Carole, may the creative spark God has gifted you with be used for His glory. I'm humbled and eternally grateful the Lord chose me to be your mom.

To Mom: Over the years, you have been "mom" and "dad." Many times, and for many seasons, you have endured the hardships of keeping our lives together. Through challenges and chaos, your strength has been a constant and it has made me the fearless woman I am today. Thank you for your unending support, for always showing up, and for believing in me.

To my closest friends: Katie Byrd, may the Lord bless you and keep you, friend. You are a treasure. Catherine Wehrman, may God continue to use your story, and your heart for Him, to revive a generation and call His church to attention. Laura Early, may the Lord of Hosts give you the gift of seeing just how much of His kingdom you have been a part of building. Lindsey Litton, may He who began a good work in you bring it to completion. Andi Adams, may the God who sees remind you always of His faithfulness and send His Spirit to comfort your soul. Jess Manfre, may Our Father in Heaven spur you forward as you serve Him with fervor.

For my Mentors: Lita Norsworthy, Galen has left a legacy of love and devotion. This legacy is most certainly alive and well in your care and compassion for all of us in the military spouse community. I love you dearly. Dr. Gloria Grell, your unending encouragement and instruction is such an immense blessing to me. Meeting you at the Called Conference in 2017 changed my life and you have spoken such life into me. Thank you. Erica Wiggenhorn, thank you for continuing to speak with me after the insane amount of fangirling, freakouts, and fanatical phone calls. You are a complete embodiment of what I believe a woman in ministry should be. Thank you for showing me what it means to be unwaveringly faithful to gospel missions. Endel Lee, I hope I am half the leader you are "when I grow up." Your encouragement, mission training, and caring mentorship means more to me than I could ever express in words. Your faithfulness to the Lord and His gospel work will always inspire me.

To our Family Pastors: Adam Bennett, what a pleasure it is to co-labor for Christ at Back Bay Church. Thank you for giving my family a home and shepherding us well. To Chaplain Steve Dabbs, you forever changed the course of our lives when you took a risk on some punk Bible teacher and launched me into ministry. Your example of ministry leadership and impeccable character will always guide me as I continue to serve the military community. Thank you for your investment in me and your belief in our mission.

Justin Daniel, this book is just another piece of evidence that your willingness to disciple military spouses has paid dividends. Your friendship is a gift, and so many of us in this community have benefited from your shepherding. Each of you have made the flame in our hearts for evangelism glow a little brighter.

Last, but certainly not least, to the amazing women at Moody Publishers who have invested so much in me, nurtured my soul, and have made me a better writer and leader, thank you. Judy Dunagan, your belief in me is a constant source of confidence and urges me to follow your example of following Christ fully. This new line of military contextualized books has been a dream of mine and a persistent part of what I have asked God for over the last several years. Your heart to serve women all over the globe, including the women in my community, truly will have an immeasurable impact on the kingdom of heaven. Your friendship is certainly one of God's greatest gifts to me. Pam Pugh, without you, I'm not sure many would be able to discern much from me through all of the sarcasm and slang that comes so naturally to my writing. Indeed, I am a more capable communicator because of your tender correction, practical instruction, and the wellspring of patience you have with me through the editing process. You are a treasure.

Notes

1. "Strong's Concordance: 3341 *metanoia*," Bible Hub, https://biblehub.com/greek/3341.htm.

2. "Strong's Concordance: 4102 *pistis*," Bible Hub, https://biblehub.com/greek/4102.htm.

3. Gary Chapman and Jocelyn Green, *The 5 Love Languages Military Edition: The Secret to Love That Lasts* (Chicago: Northfield Publishing, 2017). Visit 5lovelanguages.com for more information and a fun quiz.

4. H. G. Liddell, Robert Scott, and Henry Stuart Jones, "Agape," in *A Greek-English Lexicon* (Oxford: Clarendon Press, 1996).

See also "Strong's Concordance: 26 *agapé*," Bible Hub, https://biblehub.com/greek/26.htm.

5. Michael Vanlaningham, "Matthew," in *The Moody Bible Commentary*, eds. Michael Rydelnik and Michael Vanlaningham (Chicago: Moody Publishers, 2014), 1514.

6. Erica Wiggenhorn, *Unexplainable Jesus: Rediscovering the God You Thought You Knew* (Chicago: Moody Publishers, 2019).

ENCOUNTER THE FULLNESS OF GOD'S GRACE,
THE POWER OF HIS PROMISES, AND THE BEAUTY
OF HIS FAITHFULNESS—ALL THROUGH THE LIFE
OF ONE WOMAN: ESTHER.

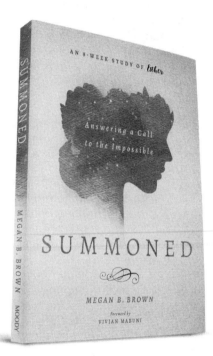

FARAWAY LANDS, FEAR, AND FAITH— RUTH PAVES THE WAY FOR OUR STORY.

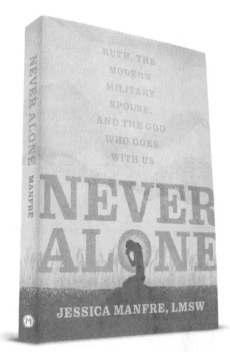

If your spouse or someone you know has been deployed recently, the stress of this situation will resonate with you.

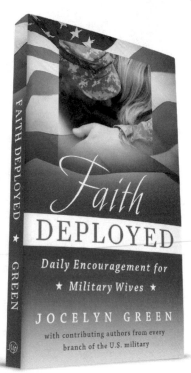

ADVICE FOR MILITARY COUPLES

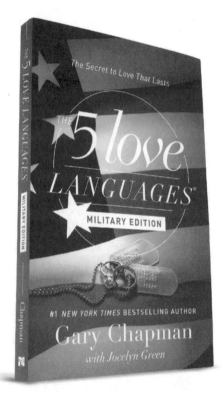

The #1 *New York Times* bestseller *The 5 Love Languages*® has transformed millions of marriages. Now military couples can enjoy their own version of this classic book. Dr. Gary Chapman and author and former military wife Jocelyn Green share insights on how to use the love languages during deployment—and much more.

978-0-8024-1482-3 | also available as an eBook and audiobook